Gandhi

Gandhi

Amy Pastan

DK Publishing

LONDON, NEW YORK, MUNICH,
MELBOURNE, AND DELHI

Editor : Alisha Niehaus
Editorial Assistant : John Searcy
Publishing Director : Beth Sutinis
Senior Designer : Tai Blanche
Art Director : Dirk Kaufman
Design : T. Reitzle/Oxygen Design
Photo Research : Anne Burns Images
Production : Ivor Parker
DTP Designer : Kathy Farias

First American Edition, 2006

06 07 08 09 10 10 9 8 7 6 5 4 3 2 1
Published in the United States
by DK Publishing
375 Hudson Street, New York, New York 10014

Published in Great Britain by Dorling Kindersley Limited.

DK books are available at special discounts for bulk purchases for sales
promotions, premiums, fund-raising, or educational use.
For details, contact:
DK Publishing Special Markets
375 Hudson Street, New York, NY 10014
SpecialSales@dk.com

A catalog record for this book is available
from the Library of Congress.

ISBN-10 0-7566-2111-9 ISBN-13 978-0-7566-2111-7 (paperback)
ISBN-10 0-7566-2112-7 ISBN-13 978-0-7566-2112-4 (hardcover)

Color reproduction by GRB Editrice, Italy
Printed and bound in China by
South China Printing Co., Ltd.

Photography credits:
Cover Photo by Alamy Images/Dinodia Images
Back Cover Photo by Corbis/Bettman

Discover more at
www.dk.com

Contents

chapter **1**

Gandhi's India

For Mohandas Gandhi, a small and unassuming man who became the heart and soul of India in the 20th century, truth was all important. Even as a schoolboy, he feared telling a lie. When he misspelled the word *kettle* during the education inspector's visit in high school, his teacher secretly prodded him with the point of his boot, hoping to prompt Gandhi to copy the correct spelling from his neighbor's slate. But Gandhi could not understand why the teacher was kicking him. It would never have occurred to him to use the work of another student. So, while the rest of the class sailed through the exercise, Gandhi stumbled. Later in life, this same love for truth and his stubborn attachment to it would spur him to lead millions of Indians in a fight for independence from British rule. It was a fight without weapons, because for Gandhi truth was stronger than a sword.

Gandhi led nonviolent protests well into his old age and became a symbol of hope for future generations.

Mohandas Karamchand Gandhi was born in Porbandar, India on October 2, 1869. At this time, despite strong British influence on the country's politics, religious traditions were the most important aspect of everyday Indian life. The Gandhis followed the Hindu religion, as did a majority of Indians. Muslims were the other main religious group, making up approximately 20 percent of India's population.

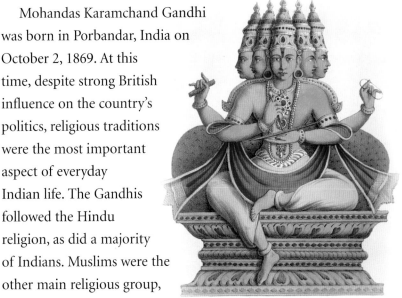

Brahma, who takes many forms, is depicted here with five heads and four arms.

Hindus and Muslims have very different beliefs. Muslims worship Allah as their only god, while Hindus believe that God takes many different forms. These forms are called deities. Some of the most popular Hindu deities are Brahma, Vishnu, and Krishna. Hindus believe that God is omnipresent—he exists everywhere and in all living things. Muslims forbid the representation of God in any form. There are no paintings or statues of Allah. The Muslims' holy book is the Koran, written in Arabic. For Hindus the Bhagavad Gita and the Ramayana are the most common sacred texts. They are written in Sanskrit, a classical Indian language. Hindus consider the cow to be

BONFIRE OF FOREIGN CLOTHES
Shall take place at the Maidan near Elphinstone Mills, Opp. Elphinstone Road Station on Sunday, 31st July, 1921.
THE CEREMONY WILL BE PERFORMED BY
MAHATMA GANDHIJI
All are requested to attend in Swadeshi Clothes of Khadi. Those who have not given away their Foreign Clothes are requested to bring them to the Maidan.
SPECIAL ARRANGEMENT IS MADE FOR LADIES AND CHILDREN
IN HONOUR OF
LOKMANYA TILAK
ATTORNEY

sacred and some Hindus are strict vegetarians—they refrain from eating meat. Muslims shun pork, but will eat beef. The religious diversity of India, which included Hindus, Muslims, Buddhists, Jews, Christians, and Parsis, who spoke dozens of languages and hundreds of dialects, made Gandhi's later achievement—uniting all Indians against the British government—extraordinary.

When Gandhi was young, his father, Karamchand, became *diwan,* or prime minister, of the Rajkot State. Karamchand's father and brother had also been

Key

Princely states

Ruled directly by Britain

diwans. Although India was part of the British Empire in the late 1800s, local princes were allowed to stay in power in their regions as long as they obeyed the viceroy, the highest British official in India. The diwans assisted these princes. Gandhi's father was not well educated, but he was skilled at managing people and settling disputes. His experience—and his caste— made him a respected member

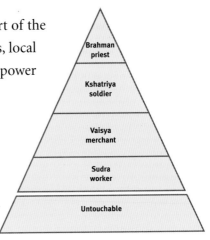

This chart shows the Hindu caste system. Within each caste there are thousands of subcastes, which vary from region to region.

of Indian society. Gandhi's family hoped Mohandas would become a diwan, too, someday.

Because the Gandhis were Hindu, they belonged to a particular caste, or group. A caste originally indicated one's job in society. A Hindu might have been born a Brahman (priest), a Kshatriya (soldier), a Vaisya (merchant), or a Sudra (worker). Those who did the lowest tasks, such as collecting garbage or cleaning latrines, were without caste. They were called untouchables. They were not permitted to worship with or mix with people who had castes, but had their own shrines and temples. Gandhi's family was of the Vaisya caste.

PARSI

A Parsi is a member of the Zoroastrian sect, which came to India from Persia in the 7th or 8th century.

9

Long before Gandhi's birth, India was home to many ancient cultures. The earliest known civilization in India was the Indus Valley Civilization, which

These excavations of the ancient city of Mohenjo Daro reveal the ruins of Indus Civilization baths.

appeared around 3000 BC. These highly developed people had a written language, complex cities, and sophisticated water systems that included baths and household toilets. New settlers moved in from the north in 1500 BC. They were called Aryans. The Aryans farmed, raised cattle, wrote in Sanskrit, and introduced a social system that became the foundation of India's castes.

In the 5th century BC, many new religious sects were emerging in India. Siddhartha Gautama founded the religion of Buddhism, which is still widely practiced in

India as well as around the world. Alexander the Great's armies briefly swept through the northwest in about 330 BC, but did not stay

long. The first time the country became united was under King Candragupta, who, in about 321 BC, founded one of India's great dynasties: the Maurya. The most memorable Maurya king was Ashoka, who conquered nearly the entire subcontinent. When the Maurya dynasty ended, India divided into smaller kingdoms and was plagued for centuries by bloody takeovers.

Babur, a Muslim monarch, became the founder of the Mogul dynasty in the early 16th century. He was a warrior, but he also loved poetry, gardening, and books. After Babur's death, his grandson, Akbar, extended their empire through massacres in which more than one million Hindus were killed. Akbar, too, had a passion for books, and his great library had volumes in many languages,

This horoscope of an Indian prince is written in Sanskrit. The language's status in India is similar to that of Latin and Greek in Europe.

including Hindi, Persian, Greek, Kashmiri, English, and Arabic. The reign of Akbar's son Jahan-gir is remembered through beautiful paintings depicting political events and colorful scenes of lavish court life. Jahan-gir's son Shah Jahan was responsible for leaving behind stunning architectural monuments. The most famous building he erected was the Taj Mahal, built as a tomb for his beloved wife Mumtaz Mahal.

Under the ruthless regimes of the next Mogul ruler Aurangzeb (1618–1707) and his successors, Hindus who feared losing their traditions began to resist their Muslim masters.

The Taj Mahal remains one of India's most impressive sites.

At the same time, the costs of the Moguls' rich lifestyles and expensive military campaigns began to add up, and there was not enough money to support the people. Thus, the power of the Mogul Empire began to dwindle just as Europeans— primarily Portuguese, Dutch, and British—began to profit from the subcontinent's rich resources.

The Dutch East India Company (whose insignia is shown here) established early posts in India, but its power was later eclipsed by the British.

In fact, by this time, the British had already been the dominant European presence in India for more than two hundred years. Originally lured by money to be made in the spice market, British merchants had formed the East India Trading Company in 1599. A few years later, its first ship docked in Surat, just north of Bombay. The newcomers presented themselves at the court of the Mogul leader, Jahan-gir. The British managed to persuade their host to sign an agreement allowing the East India Company to establish trading depots in India. Soon boats loaded with pepper, indigo, cinnamon, silk, and sugar headed back with wares for London's finest shops.

The British claimed that their goal was trade, not conquest. But this policy abruptly changed in the mid-1700s when a few ambitious British governors used their armies to claim Indian kingdoms in the name of the British Empire.

The Battle of Plassey on June 23, 1757, was the turning point in British policy toward India. Prior to the conflict, disagreements between the Nawab (Indian deputy) of Bengal and the East India Company had been growing for many years. Tensions finally came to a head when the Nawab's army attacked a British camp near Calcutta. However, British Colonel Robert Clive soundly defeated the Nawab's troops, after which the British started steadily building up their military might in India. They no longer sought to be visiting traders, but permanent rulers.

The British skillfully infiltrated the courts and kingdoms of India through clever treaties with native princes. They hired Indian soldiers in their regiments and acquired great power. But the people of India began to suspect the motives of the British. Many devout Hindus and Muslims were worried that their European rulers would try to convert them to Christianity or force them to eat meat or pork. Even the Indian troops recruited by the British did not trust their leaders. Their year-long rebellion against their British officers, the Mutiny of 1857, ended in

Lord Clive, British hero of the Battle of Plassey, receives a grant of money for injured soldiers.

British Imperialism

British imperialism was the result of the competition for trade between England, Spain, France, and Holland. These nations wanted goods from places such as Turkey, Africa, and the East Indies, where they could buy cheap spices, cotton, and silk to sell for a profit back home. British rulers and merchants wanted to keep all this wealth in their Empire. So wars were waged to defeat competitors, and foreign lands, such as India, were conquered to achieve that goal. The Empire eventually became so large that the sun was always shining in some part of it, giving rise to the phrase "The sun never sets on the British Empire."

a loss for India. The British finally gained total control of the country in 1858, just 11 years before Mohandas Gandhi was born. How a small island nation thousands of miles away could hold power over the lives of 300 million people was a source of wonder to many. Gandhi would one day pledge to take this power away from the British and return it to the people of India.

The British government in India was called the Raj. By Gandhi's time, it controlled the entire subcontinent,

including areas now known as Pakistan, Bangladesh, and Burma. In 1877, Queen Victoria of England took on the title Empress of India, yet Victoria herself never visited India. She trusted her viceroy to represent her interests there.

Meanwhile, Indian goods continued to make Britain very wealthy, and the English referred to India as "the jewel in the crown." One of the most desired materials from India was raw cotton, which was shipped back to England where it was made into colorful cloth. Some dyed cloth was then sent back to India, where women bought it to make flowing dresses called *saris*. Many Indians resented paying high prices for cloth that originally came from their own country. While the British grew richer, poverty in India was widespread.

The impact of British rule on daily life was felt in ways beyond government and trade—and it was not always bad for Indians. In their efforts to

A crowd of people—some riding elephants—attend the opening of the East Indian Railway in Calcutta.

promote their trade interests, the British made many improvements. They built an extraordinary railroad system that linked the major regions of India. This improved communication and travel throughout the massive territory. In addition, English became the common language for people who spoke different regional languages. Thus, even as the spread of English helped the British dominate a nation that had more than a dozen tongues and hundreds of dialects, at the same time it allowed Indians who spoke different languages to communicate with each

Queen Victoria (1817–1901)

Queen Victoria was the longest-reigning monarch in the history of Britain. She became queen at the age of 18 and held the throne until her death at the age of 81. Victoria's reign coincided with the expansion of the British Empire and the beginning of the machine age, known as the Industrial Revolution. This time in history is often called the Victorian era.

other. For the first time, a Hindi speaker had an easy way to communicate with an Urdu speaker in another town. Although Gandhi spoke Gujarati at home, he learned to speak, read, and write English at school. He would skillfully employ his acquired language to gain rights for his countrymen.

chapter 2

Growing Up in Gujarat

Mohandas was raised in a privileged household. His father, the diwan, had two daughters from earlier marriages, and a daughter and three sons from his marriage to Putliba, Gandhi's mother. Putliba was deeply religious and regularly observed periods of fasting. Many Hindus believe that fasting clears the mind and strengthens one's control over material desires. From Putliba, Gandhi learned the importance of keeping one's vows. Once, during the rainy season, she vowed not to eat until the sun appeared. Her children anxiously kept their eyes on the sky, but Putliba waited patiently through cloudy days. She would not weaken.

Gandhi's father, Karamchand, had little religious training, but because Hindu culture was part of everyday life, he absorbed many of the teachings of Hindu religious texts, such as the Bhagavad Gita. Often short-tempered, but remembered by his youngest son as a proud and generous father, Karamchand was called to the city of Rajkot when Mohandas was seven to serve in the local prince's court. There, Mohandas attended primary school.

Gandhi was born in this house in Porbandar, India.

School had always been a painful experience for young Gandhi. In Rajkot, as at his first school in Porbandar, he was not an outstanding student. Small for his age and very skinny, he had ears that stuck out awkwardly from his head. Constantly fearful of being teased for his looks, Gandhi ran to school each morning, arriving just in time for class to begin. As soon as lessons were over in the afternoon, he fled back home, hoping that no one would see him.

Gandhi adored his mother, Putliba, and wrote that the ladies of the court "thought highly of her intelligence."

At the age of 12, Gandhi entered high school. There, all classes were taught in English rather than the regional language, Gujarati. Gandhi found learning geometry particularly difficult. He also had trouble with Sanskrit, the ancient language of the Hindu religious texts. Hearing that Persian was easier, he snuck into that class instead one day. The Sanskrit teacher, appalled that Mohandas—a member of the respected Vaisya caste—would drop the language of his religion, convinced the boy to give Sanskrit another try. Gandhi was forever grateful for his teacher's patience. Later in life, Gandhi mastered Hindi, Gujarati, Sanskrit, and English, and believed that

In this photograph, the earliest known image of Gandhi, he was seven years old.

schoolchildren in India should learn Hindi, Sanskrit, Persian, and Arabic, along with their regional languages.

In high school, Gandhi began to make friends. One of his companions was a strong boy named Sheik Mehtab, who was healthy and athletic. He was a great high jumper. The weak-bodied Gandhi hated physical exercise and was impressed by his classmate. Despite the warnings of his mother and oldest brother that Sheik could be a bad influence, Gandhi grew close to the boy. He felt that he had the inner strength to resist any temptations Sheik or others might offer.

For Gandhi's family, eating meat was a great taboo. But Gandhi's new friend begged him to try it. He told Gandhi that eating meat made one healthy and strong. He argued that the English ate

Alfred High School, which Gandhi attended, is still in Rajkot. It is now called Mahatma Gandhi High School.

meat and that was why they had power over all of India. The logic of this impressed Gandhi, who even in high school was so timid that he was afraid of the dark. Imagining that serpents, ghosts, and thieves would emerge from the blackness of his room, he slept with the lights on. So, when his companion proposed meat-eating as a way to combat these demons, Gandhi gave in. Soon, shame overcame him. He saw that giving in to peer pressure meant having to lie to his family, and he gave up meat for good.

Gandhi, left, is pictured with a high school classmate. The photo was taken in 1883 when Gandhi was 14 years old.

It was also around this time that Gandhi became fascinated with smoking, even going so far as to steal change from the household servants to buy cigarettes. His greater offense, however, was to steal gold from his brother, who owed a debt of 25 rupees (about $200 in today's money). Gandhi used the gold to pay off his irresponsible brother's debt—but in so doing, he committed a crime that weighed heavily on his conscience. Gandhi wrote a confession to his father and asked him for the greatest punishment possible. He thought his father, who was capable of becoming very angry, would be very harsh with him, but the diwan was moved to tears by his son's repentance. For young Gandhi, such understanding from a loving parent was a

lesson he never forgot. Later in life, when his countrymen gave
him the title *Mahatma* or "Great Soul," Gandhi remembered
with some embarrassment the sins of his youth. But he also
reflected that forgiveness and compassion were gifts to those
who vowed to tell the truth. In high school, however, Gandhi
was still learning life's lessons—the most difficult of which
was how to be a husband.

It was a common practice in Gandhi's time for Hindus to
have an arranged marriage. Even today, some Hindu parents
are involved in the marriage decision, although they may not
actually pick partners for their children. When Gandhi was
young, parents promised, or betrothed, their child to another at
a very young age and the couple did not set eyes
on one another until their wedding day. Indeed,
Gandhi—only 13 years old—met
his bride, Kasturba, at their
marriage ceremony.

Hindu marriage is a sacred
and complicated ritual.
Months—sometimes years—
are spent preparing for the
big day. Much money is spent
on fine clothes, expensive
food, and lavish processions.
Mohandas's oldest brother
had already been married in

Gandhi and Kasturba, who wed as
children, had been married many years
by the time this photo was taken in 1915.

this fashion, but the second brother and a cousin close to Mohandas in age remained unattached. It was decided that it would be easier and less expensive to marry Mohandas and the other two boys off all at once rather than have three separate weddings. That was why, at such a young age, Mohandas Gandhi became a bridegroom.

Kasturba was from a prosperous family. She could not read or write, nor did she ever learn to do so, but she was a strong and patient wife. Gandhi, however, was initially a jealous teenager and difficult husband who questioned his wife's right to leave the house alone, even if she was doing so only to worship at temple or visit with friends. Fortunately, in marriages between such young people, it was customary for the bride to return to live with her parents every six months or so. These periods were a necessary break for the couple and allowed Gandhi, who had missed a whole year of high school because of his wedding, to continue his education.

Hindu Marriage Ceremony

Hindu weddings often take place in the bride's home, where a tent is erected and filled with flowers and sometimes jewels. The festivities may last for days. The most important part of the ritual is the *Saptapadi*, in which the bride and groom take seven steps around a sacred fire. With each step a vow is made. Then the couple prays for food, strength, children, and friendship.

Karamchand, Gandhi's father, taught his son to respect others.

In 1885, Gandhi was still in high school—only 16 years old, but he had the responsibilities of a man. Kasturba was expecting their first child, and his father, Karamchand, was old and very sick. Gandhi was devoted to his father and sat by his bed, massaging his legs and giving him medicine. On the night his father died, however, Gandhi had gone to spend the evening with Kasturba. He never forgave himself for being absent in his father's final moments. Sadly, Gandhi and Kasturba's baby died shortly after birth, which Gandhi saw as a punishment for being with his wife instead of tending to his father.

Gandhi had grown far more interested in Hinduism in high school and much more tolerant of different faiths as well. During his father's illness, Mohandas listened to portions of the Ramayana, an ancient Hindu epic, read aloud. His father's Muslim and Parsi friends would often visit, and the boy was exposed to their views. Gandhi observed the respect and interest his father showed to these people whose beliefs differed from his own. While Mohandas was unsure of his own feelings about God, he was making a strong commitment to morality and truth.

As his high school days ended, Gandhi prepared for college. His family hoped he would succeed his father as diwan, but times had changed

MORALITY
A moral person follows generally accepted rules of right and wrong.

since his father held the post, and a suitable education was now essential. A family advisor recommended that Mohandas go to England to become a barrister, or lawyer. Gandhi was excited by the possibility, but the prospect of leaving India was daunting. His older brother pledged to help him find the money for such an ambitious venture, but his devout mother had grave doubts about her son's plans. Putliba had heard all about England. There, according to her sources, young men ate meat, drank liquor, and were unfaithful to their wives. How could she trust her young son not to fall under the spell of Englishmen with such loose morals?

To satisfy his mother, Gandhi took a solemn vow before a Jain monk, who served as a family adviser, that he would not

This painted miniature depicts an episode from the Ramayana.

touch wine, women, or meat. Then he set off on the first leg of his trip—to Bombay. Gandhi's brother accompanied him there to help book his passage to England. They were told that it was unsafe to make ocean voyages in the summer months because the seas were very rough. So his brother left him with a friend and returned to Rajkot. Gandhi would have to bide his time alone until November. He was deeply disappointed.

Adding to the anguish of his wait were the demands of his caste. No one from the Modh Banias (the Vaisya subcaste to which Gandhi belonged) had made a trip across the ocean before. After learning of Gandhi's proposed trip, the Modh Bania elders in Bombay claimed that it was unthinkable for Gandhi to eat and drink with Europeans who did not observe the same dietary rules. They were afraid such behavior would reflect badly on their religion. Finally, Gandhi had to appear before the headman of the Modh Banias to defend himself. He cautiously explained that he had made a solemn vow to his family, which he would not break. Suddenly finding his voice, the usually timid Gandhi told the headman, "I do not think the caste should interfere in the matter." With that, the

OUTCASTE

In India, the word "outcaste" means a person expelled from or without a caste, and was first used by the British to describe Indians who had violated caste laws.

headman declared, "I think this boy should be treated as an outcaste from today."

Fearful that his family would suffer for his outspokenness, Gandhi wrote his brother and told him what the headman had said. His brother assured him that he had the family's blessing. So, with the help of friends, Gandhi arranged to depart for England before any other mishaps could occur. He sailed on September 4, 1888. He was 18 years old. In his luggage were new clothes, more suitable for the British climate and more appropriate in style. Gandhi prized the clean white flannel suit and saved it the entire journey so he could wear it ashore when the boat arrived. However, when the ship docked in Southampton, England, in late September, Gandhi was like a white spot in a sea of black—the only passenger to wear summer clothes so late in the season. He would soon discover that more than his clothes set him apart from others in his temporary home.

The ship on which Gandhi sailed to England, the *SS Clyde*, would have looked similar to this ship, which was from the same fleet.

chapter 3

An Indian Abroad

Even though he had grown up under British rule in India, nothing had prepared Gandhi for the strangeness of England. In day-to-day life in Rajkot, he had experienced little interaction with English people. Indians lived apart from British society, and most were servants or soldiers. The sea voyage had already shaken Gandhi. He was not accustomed to speaking English all the time and shyness prevented him from trying. He didn't know how to use a knife and fork properly because it wasn't the custom where he was from, and he couldn't tell if the meals contained meat—nor did he dare to ask. It was safer to keep to his cabin.

However, once on land, there was nowhere to hide. Gandhi spent sleepless nights in his rented rooms,

The dome of St. Paul's Cathedral rises from Fleet Street in this view of London in the 1890s.

crying with homesickness: "Everything was strange," he later wrote, "the people, their ways, and even their dwellings. I was a complete novice in the matter of English etiquette and continually had to be on my guard. There was the additional inconvenience of the vegetarian vow. Even the dishes I could eat were tasteless and insipid."

Food became an all-consuming issue for Gandhi. He was practically starving and was too ashamed to ask his landlady for extra servings of bread. But Gandhi would not violate the vow made to his mother. Fortunately, he came across a vegetarian restaurant in Farringdon Street during one of his walks through the city. He was overjoyed to eat his first satisfying meal since his arrival in Britain. In the window, the restaurant displayed a copy of Henry Stephens Salt's *A Plea for Vegetarianism*, which Gandhi promptly bought.

Despite his misgivings about having tried meat in high school, Gandhi had always wished that he could be a meat-eater. He was not a vegetarian by choice, but by obligation. His effort to live a truthful life meant that he could not break the restrictions required by his religion or turn back on his promise to his mother. So Salt's book, which explained the healthy benefits of a vegetarian diet and explored the philosophy of vegetarianism, was exciting news. It encouraged

At age 18, Gandhi was heading to law school and had already adopted the European style of dress.

Vegetarian Society

Henry Stephens Salt (1851–1939) was a noted British writer and pacifist who supported reforms to improve conditions in schools and prisons. He also believed in the fair treatment of animals and was devoted to the vegetarian lifestyle. His first book, *A Plea for Vegetarianism,* was published by the Vegetarian Society of Britain in 1886. The society, of which Gandhi later became a member (he designed the society's logo, above), was founded in 1847.

Gandhi to read other books on the subject and to investigate the physical and mental benefits of living without meat. He was able to resist his meat-eating friends' attempts to "reform" him with greater conviction. When he was older, this conviction would take on more of a religious meaning for Gandhi.

Realizing that his diet made him different, Gandhi found other ways to blend into his new environment. He was still hurting from the shame of his white suit and set out to find more fashionable clothes than those he had brought from Bombay. He asked his older brother to send him a gold watch chain and began to part his unruly hair. There had been no mirrors in his home in India, but mirrors were commonplace in England; he could take his time checking and rechecking his appearance before venturing into society.

Gandhi acquired a top hat, evening suit, and walking stick, but knew there was more to becoming a proper English

gentleman. Despite his strict budget, he signed up for dance lessons, which he soon quit, as he could not "achieve anything like rhythmic motion." Thinking the violin might be a better choice, he invested in an instrument and teacher. He even attended elocution, or speech, classes. Gandhi eventually came to see the foolishness and waste in these pursuits. He would not be spending the rest of his life in England, only a few years. He decided that "if my character made a gentleman of me, so much the better," and focused on his studies.

Gandhi, seated front right, poses with members of the Vegetarian Society in 1890.

The courses at University College London were not easy. In addition to the bar exam, Gandhi hoped to pass difficult tests in Latin, French, and chemistry. At the same time, he changed his lifestyle to live less expensively. He had roomed

BONFIRE OF FOREIGN CLOTHES

Shall take place at the Maidan near Elphinstone Mills
Opp. Elphinstone Road Station on Sunday, 31st July, 1921.
THE CEREMONY WILL BE PERFORMED BY

MAHATMA GANDHIJI

All are requested to attend in Swadeshi Clothes of Khadi. Those who have at
given away their Foreign Clothes are requested to bring them to the Meeting
SPECIAL ARRANGEMENT IS MADE FOR LADIES
AND CHILDREN
PRESIDED BY

LOKMANYA TILAK

ATTORNEY

Bhagavad Gita

The Bhagavad Gita is an epic poem of 700 verses and serves as a guide to the Self, the Universe, and the Supreme. The story tells of a battle between the Pandava brothers and the Kauravas, their cousins, who cheated the brothers of their rightful kingdom. When one Pandava brother, Arjuna the Mighty Warrior, sees his kinsmen ready to sacrifice their lives in battle he is overcome by grief and loses the will to fight. Arjuna confides his weakness to his charioteer, who is really Lord Krishna—a divine being—in disguise. Krishna urges Arjuna to obtain knowledge, take action regardless of the outcome, and devote himself to God. Krishna's teachings persuade Arjuna to fight. In the end, the god reveals his true self to Arjuna. There are many translations of this epic, including one by Gandhi in his native language, Gujarati.

with a family to whom he paid rent, but decided to find his own place, which was cheaper. He stopped paying for transportation and began to walk everywhere, even if he was going 10 miles (16 kilometers) away. He cut expenses, existing on porridge and cocoa for breakfast and dinner. He knew that his family back in India had made many sacrifices so he could have this opportunity. He did not want to keep

asking them for
money. And what
Gandhi discovered
was that the
simpler life was a
more truthful life.
He was not sorry to
give up the things he
did not need. Actually,
it made him happy.

During his stay in England Gandhi began
to learn more about his own religion, as
well as about other faiths. He joined the

Theosophists are
interested in a wide
range of religions
and cultures.

Vegetarian Society and became acquainted with a group
called the Theosophists. The Theosophists studied all
religions and tried to find common threads among them.
They read sacred texts to gain a better understanding of
people's beliefs. The Theosophists hoped that Gandhi would
join them in reading the Bhagavad Gita.

Gandhi had not read the Gita in India, nor was his
knowledge of Sanskrit up to the task. But his friends
assured him that the Gita could be enjoyed in English,
recommending a translation by Sir Edwin Arnold. Gandhi
fell in love with Sir Edwin's translation, which was easy
to read and highly poetic. In later years, Gandhi would
read the Gita daily. Although he never formally joined the
Theosophists, the group exposed him to the larger world

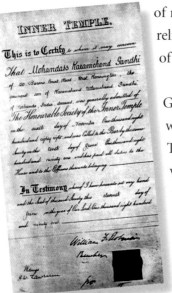

INNER TEMPLE.

This is to Certify to whom it may concern

That Mohandass Karamchand Gandhi

...

This Bar-at-Law certificate was granted to Gandhi in 1891.

of religion and offered an example of religious tolerance that became part of his message as a Mahatma.

It was in Britain as well that Gandhi first became acquainted with the Bible, particularly the New Testament, which delighted him. One verse in particular reminded him of the Gita: "But I say unto you, that ye resist not evil: but whosoever shall smite thee on thy cheek, turn to him the other also. And if any man take away thy coat, let him have thy cloke too." The concept of renunciation captivated him. He would pledge himself to it as a way to please God and win rights for the poor and abused in years to come.

Gandhi was finally ready to take his law examinations and be "called to the bar" or become a lawyer. He passed his exams on June 10, 1891, and wasted no time departing from the temporary home where he had suffered much but also learned a good deal. On June 12, he sailed for India.

The summer seas were rough, and Gandhi himself was at sea about his future. He was nervous about how to actually practice the profession he had studied. He had no experience. He was scared, too, about

RENUNCIATION

Renunciation is the act of giving up or disowning something.

34

confronting the caste that had rejected him when he went to England, and he was probably anxious about reuniting with Kasturba and his son, Harilal, who had been born shortly before he left India and was now almost four years old. But his spirits soared at the prospect of seeing his mother. After all, he had kept his vows and become even more devoted to his religion in England. He was returning home a different man— more bound to the truth and more interested in reform.

Gandhi arrived in Bombay to his brother's embraces and a terrible shock—his mother had died just weeks before. No one had wanted to tell him the bad news while he was so far away. Though grieved even more than he had been by his father's death, Gandhi did not have time to give in to sadness. His brother had been eager for his return. He was counting on his younger sibling—now a British-trained lawyer—to bring the family wealth and fame. In anticipation of Gandhi's return, he had overspent the household budget on luxuries such as tea, coffee, and European clothes. Gandhi would have to find work quickly to support such extravagances.

Gandhi succeeded in becoming a British barrister.

The truth was that his studies in Britain had not prepared Gandhi to practice law in India. Indian law and courts were different from those in England, so Gandhi established a household in Bombay where he could study Indian law and make connections. He made his debut as a lawyer in small cases court. His first case was not a big one, but when it came time for Gandhi to cross-examine the opposing side's witness, his mind went blank. He did not have the courage to speak up in the courtroom and fled the proceedings in shame.

It was back in Rajkot that Gandhi came face-to-face with British authority for the first time. Gandhi's

This British officer wears the outfit of a major in India during this period.

brother had gotten into some legal trouble. He was hoping to clear his name with the local political agent (a British official in charge of the region) and asked Gandhi, who had met the agent in England, to help him out. Gandhi realized that it was wrong to ask political favors of personal acquaintances. Still, he could not refuse his brother.

Gandhi sought, and got, an appointment to see the agent. But the man he encountered in India was different from the

man he remembered from England. In Britain, the agent had been on leave from his post and was fairly friendly. In India, he was a British

officer—a sahib—on duty. The previous acquaintance meant nothing here. Worse yet, he refused to listen to Gandhi's plea on his brother's behalf. When Gandhi persisted, the officer called in his servant and had Gandhi physically dragged from the room.

The insult was great and Gandhi was crushed. Thinking to take action against the sahib, he contacted a well-established lawyer for advice. The lawyer advised that there was nothing to be gained by filing a complaint against the British officer—Gandhi would most likely ruin himself in the process. Gandhi later wrote that "the advice was bitter as poison to me, but I had to swallow it. I pocketed the insult, but also profited by it. 'Never again shall I place myself in such a false position, never again shall I try to exploit friendship this way,' said I to myself and since then I have never been guilty of a breach of that determination. This shock changed the course of my life."

Gandhi was not only humiliated by this event, but put in a bad position. Naturally, if he were to work in the local court, he would encounter this officer. He had no desire to meet him again nor to become involved in the power struggles between the British sahibs and local politicians. He was just beginning to get desperate about his future when an interesting offer came his way.

37

chapter 4

Finding a Voice

Gandhi's sense of frustration and failure as an attorney in India quickly turned to anticipation. Through contacts of his brother, he received a job offer from the law firm of Dada Abdulla and Company. The company had a big case in South Africa and thought Gandhi would be a useful assistant there. Of course, it was not so easy for Gandhi to leave Rajkot. He and Kasturba had recently had another child—a son, Manilal. The company required a commitment of a year. Still, he needed the income to support his family and the opportunity seemed too good to refuse. He sailed for Durban, in the South African state

Horse-drawn vehicles were commonly seen on West Street in Durban, South Africa in 1895.

of Natal, in April 1893. In England he had come to accept his culture and religion; in South Africa he would find the voice to defend them.

The ship docked in Durban at the end of May. Abdulla Sheth, a representative of the law firm, was there to meet him. Although Gandhi's clothes did not raise as many eyebrows as his white flannel suit had in England years before, he was clearly conspicuous in a European-style frock coat and Indian turban. As people came on board to greet their friends, Gandhi sensed that the

Gandhi's turban started a scandal.

Indians were treated differently than other people. He was uncomfortable with the lack of respect they were shown. Abdulla Sheth, however, was welcoming. Sheth, a Muslim, took Gandhi, a Hindu newcomer, under his wing. He introduced him to the Indian community and presented him at the Durban court.

The racial divide experienced by Indians in South Africa became all too clear to Gandhi within just days of his arrival.

INDENTURED LABORER

An indentured laborer is a person bound by a contract to work for another.

Most Indians living there had come to the country as indentured laborers to the white ruling class.

Although they were Muslims, Hindus, and Parsis, Indians were treated as one lowly group called "coolies." Merchants were called "coolie merchants." Gandhi, a lawyer, was called a "coolie barrister." Gandhi was already feeling the disapproval of the white classes when he entered the court, but when the magistrate asked him to remove his turban, he became angry. Unwilling to fulfill the magistrate's request, Gandhi walked out. Afterwards, he wrote to the newspaper defending the wearing of turbans in court. The press criticized the "unwelcome visitor," but some people supported him, and the turban remained part of Gandhi's attire.

The look and feel of South African courtrooms were patterned after courtrooms in England.

It was the first of many times Gandhi would use the press to promote his views.

After a short stay in Durban, Gandhi was sent to join the firm's other lawyers in Pretoria. A first-class ticket was purchased for him. When the train made an evening stop in Maritzburg, a white passenger boarded. He was clearly uncomfortable about sharing a first-class compartment with a "colored" man and called the railway officials to deal with the matter. They asked Gandhi to move to a third-class seat. Gandhi refused. He had a first-class ticket, which entitled him to stay, he argued. The railway officials then called in a policeman, who lifted Gandhi and his luggage from the seat and physically pushed them out the train. Gandhi watched the locomotive steam away from the platform.

South Africa

In the 1890s, when Gandhi arrived, South Africa had four states—the Orange Free State, Transvaal, Natal, and Cape Colony, all of which were controlled by the British or the Boers. The Boers were the descendents of white settlers of Dutch, German, or Flemish origin. Of the approximately 75,000 Indians in South Africa at that time, many worked for low wages on British-owned coffee, tea, and sugar plantations.

It was winter in South Africa. In the bitterly cold waiting room at Maritzburg, Gandhi had time to think. The station authorities had picked up Gandhi's luggage in which he'd packed his coat. He was too proud to ask for his case, so he

41

Signs like this reminded Indians of their low status in South African society.

shivered and considered his options: "Should I fight for my rights and go back to India, or should I go on to Pretoria without minding the insults, and return to India after finishing the case?" He decided to go on to Pretoria to finish the work he had promised to do. But he also made a pledge to himself—to fight the "deep disease of color prejudice." He knew he would suffer hardships while doing so—and he was prepared.

Gandhi sent a telegram to the railway management complaining about his treatment. In the meantime, he was booked on another train to Pretoria. In Charlestown he got off and switched to a stagecoach bound for Johannesburg. Again, he ran into problems. Although Gandhi had a ticket for the coach, he was told that it had been canceled. Gandhi was anxious to get to Pretoria. He could not miss the coach. But he knew now why there was no seat for him. Only white passengers were seated in the coach, and Gandhi was a "coolie."

Gandhi resigned himself to sitting on a box outside with the coachman while the white conductor sat inside with the white

travelers. He no longer had any doubts about what life was like for Indians in South Africa. Someone would have to speak up on their behalf. It was on that long miserable trip to Pretoria that Gandhi sensed he might become their spokesman.

While Gandhi worked on the trial in Pretoria, he began to make connections with the Indian community. The first public speech he ever made was to local merchants about "truthfulness in business," but Gandhi expanded on the topic, explaining the importance of living a truthful life. He also stressed the necessity of coming together as a group, despite their varied faiths—Hindu, Parsi, Muslim, Christian—and urged them to learn English so they could better represent themselves in South African society.

Gandhi researched South African history and the social, political, and economic conditions of Indians in South Africa. He learned about the limited trades Indians could

Gandhi (standing in the back row, seventh from right) formed a soccer team of passive resisters in 1913.

legally practice, about the taxes they were required to pay, and about their daily restrictions—they were not allowed outdoors after 9:00 PM without a permit. He also experienced injustices firsthand. Still, Gandhi felt his year's stay in Pretoria had been a crucial turning point in his life. There he acquired a true knowledge of the law and, as he later wrote, "The religious spirit within me became a living force."

Gandhi sits in front of his Durban law office with staff members, including his clerk, H.S.L. Polak, on the left, and his Russian assistant, Miss Schlesen, on the right.

Gandhi headed back to Durban after the trial to prepare for the trip home. Just before he sailed, however, he read in the paper about the Indian Franchise Bill. If passed, this law would deprive Indians of their right to elect members of the Natal Legislative Assembly—they would have no representation in local government. Gandhi thought the bill was extremely dangerous: "It is the first nail into our coffin. It strikes at the root of our self respect," he told Abdulla Sheth. Gandhi was easily persuaded by his Indian colleagues to cancel his passage back to India. He would stay in South Africa and fight the Franchise Bill.

The Indians took immediate action. They sent telegrams to the all-white Legislative Assembly, as well as to the Secretary of State for the Colonies. The effort was too late—the Indians knew the bill would pass anyway—and it did. Still, the Indian community was inspired with hope and reeling with energy. Ten thousand signatures had been collected for a petition against the bill, and major newspapers in India and England had supported the Indians' cause. Gandhi was urged to stay on in Natal and continue the fight. He did not wish to accept payment for public work, but he needed a way to earn a living. Therefore, the local Indian merchants agreed to give him their private legal cases.

For the next three years Gandhi had a thriving legal practice and founded the Natal Indian Congress, which organized opposition to injustice and discrimination. Its publications were widely circulated, even in Britain, where many of the Queen's

subjects could learn, if they cared to, about people in another part of the Empire who were often governed by unjust laws fueled by prejudice.

Gandhi returned to India briefly after his second year in South Africa to fetch Kasturba and their two children. There, he tried to focus public attention on the plight of Indians in South Africa. On the return journey to Durban, their ship was quarantined—or held off shore—for health reasons. Local officials wanted to be sure that no passenger was infected with the recent plague that had swept Bombay. Gandhi learned from Abdulla Sheth, however, that he was the reason for

Kasturba joined Gandhi in South Africa, and their four sons, seen here, were raised there.

Demonstrators protested Gandhi's return to South Africa in 1897.

the quarantine. Local whites did not want him back in their country campaigning on behalf of Indians. After several days, the passengers managed to land safely. But Gandhi was met by an angry mob armed with bricks. A quick-thinking police superintendent's wife protected him from the crowd and saved him from being badly beaten.

Gandhi did not want his attackers punished. He wanted the system responsible for their actions changed, and he continued his fight for Indians in the courts and in the press. In 1899, the Boer War interrupted his work. Gandhi supported the English—because he demanded the rights of an English citizen, he felt his duty was to the Empire. He organized an all-Indian ambulance corps to tend the wounded. With more than 1,100 members, it served bravely, particularly at the bloody Battle of Spion Kop. The Indians earned praise from British officers and self-respect as well.

Boer War

Tensions between the British and the Boers (descendants of early Dutch settlers in South Africa) in Transvaal erupted into war in 1899. Called the Boer War, this conflict was provoked by Englishmen hoping to mine for gold and diamonds in Boer territory. The Boers became so angered by this intrusion that they declared war. They lost the bloody and gruesome conflict and accepted British rule, but their bitterness toward the British lasted for many years.

chapter **5**

Satyagraha in South Africa

This formal card invited guests to Gandhi's farewell party.

With his family all back under one roof, Gandhi began to experiment with the idea of self-reliance. He believed that people who perform their own tasks, rather than depending on others for help, would be more successful in facing life's challenges. He wanted to set an example for other Indians in South Africa, so even though he was wealthy enough to have servants, he learned to wash and iron his own clothes and even cut his own hair. When his third child, Ramdas, was born, Gandhi assisted with the delivery. The whole family was expected to share in all household tasks—even emptying the chamber pots. Kasturba was unhappy at having to do the work untouchables would do back in India—but in the end, she agreed with her husband's principles.

By 1901, Gandhi felt his work in South Africa was done. He wanted to go home to India. The community agreed as long as he promised to return if they needed him again. On the eve of his departure for Bombay, grateful friends showered the Gandhi family with gifts of gold, silver, and diamonds. However, Gandhi had no intention of keeping them. He would not accept

84. FIELD STREET

12 October 1901.

...favour of your presence...
...ONGRESS HALL, Grey...
...to 15th instant at 3 p.m.
...and Presentation of an...
...GANDHI. Esq.
...al for India.
...ours faithfully...
Parsee Rustomjee
Hon. Sec. Address Committee

any form of payment for public work. Kasturba felt she deserved to keep one of the necklaces. She understood that such jewelry would be out of place in her husband's household, but she wanted to have something of value to pass pn to her children. Gandhi, however, didn't agree, and she accepted his decision.

Back in India, Gandhi continued his involvement in social issues. In 1901, he attended a Calcutta meeting of the Indian National Congress, a political party dedicated to promoting the rights of Indians. He also spent time with politician Gopal Krishna Gokhale, who became an inspiration to him, as well as a close friend. In 1902, just as he was settling down into a law practice in Bombay, he received a telegram urging him to come back to Durban immediately. Joseph Chamberlain, the Secretary of State for the Colonies, would be visiting from London. Gandhi was needed to meet Mr. Chamberlain to discuss the issue of Indian rights. Sadly, the meeting for which Gandhi rushed back was a failure. Chamberlain believed that Indians should just try to

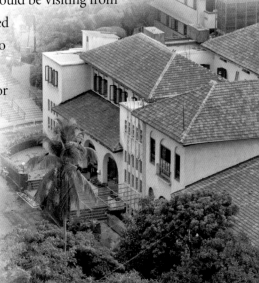

The first meeting of the Indian National Congress was held in Bombay's Tejpal Hall in 1885.

Indian Opinion

PUBLISHED WEEKLY IN ENGLISH AND GUJARATI

No. 45 · Vol. XI. WEDNESDAY NOVEMBER 12TH, 1913.

A WEEK OF EXCITEMENT

For many years the *Indian Opinion* was printed at Phoenix Settlement.

get along with Europeans in South Africa, "if you wish to live in their midst."

Disappointed but not disheartened, Gandhi pursued other ways to strengthen and unite the South African Indian community. He founded a weekly journal called the *Indian Opinion*, which featured educational articles on politics, diet, health, and sanitary habits. With the paper running smoothly, Gandhi looked for other ways to devote his life to the public good. After reading *Unto This Last*, a book by English writer John Ruskin, he was inspired to give up his possessions. Ruskin's book argued that true wealth did not mean earning more money. Richness, Ruskin believed, came with peace, not power. This idea was appealing to Gandhi, who found it similar to Hindu philosophy.

Excited by Ruskin's book, Gandhi bought a farm outside of Durban. The 90-acre Phoenix Settlement became Gandhi's first

Tolstoy Farm, 22 miles (35 kilometers) from Johannesburg, had 1,100 acres (445 hectares) of land.

Gandhi's Inspiration

John Ruskin

From John Ruskin's *Unto This Last* Gandhi learned the following principles: "1. That the good of the individual is contained in the good of all.
2. That a lawyer's work has the same value as the barber's inasmuch as all have the same right of earning their livelihood from their work.
3. That a life of labour, i.e., the life of the tiller of the soil and the handicraftsman is the life worth living."

Several other literary works also shaped Gandhi's personal philosophy, including *The Kingdom of God Within You* and *The Gospels in Brief, What To Do?* by Leo Tolstoy, and *Civil Disobedience* by Henry David Thoreau. Tolstoy, a Russian writer, inspired Gandhi to think deeply about the notion of universal love. Thoreau, an American, wrote about the value of nonviolent protest.

Henry David Thoreau

Leo Tolstoy

experimental ashram, or spiritual community. There, living first in tents with no comforts or conveniences, and then in houses made of corrugated iron, Gandhi and his followers worked, farmed, and ran the printing press for the *Indian Opinion*. Later, Gandhi would start another working colony, the Tolstoy Farm near Johannesburg. Proper hygiene and diet were important aspects of living a healthy spiritual life, and Gandhi insisted that cleanliness, natural cures for illness, and a simple vegetarian diet were maintained at his ashrams.

At his house in Johannesburg, Gandhi's family carried out the same principles that governed life in the ashrams. The children, along with Gandhi, ground flour by hand to make bread. Gandhi taught himself to make sandals. He educated his children at home, and for exercise they accompanied him on the five mile (8 kilometer) trek to his office and back.

Soon, however, Gandhi's simple life was disrupted again. The 1906 Zulu Rebellion was a series of violent skirmishes between British authorities and Natal's native Zulu population. As in the Boer War, Gandhi had no hostile feelings toward the Zulus, but as a British subject he thought it disloyal to the Empire to support them. Therefore, he again volunteered to form an Indian ambulance corps.

These are the members of the Indian volunteer ambulance corps during the Zulu Rebellion.

Once Gandhi arrived at the scene of the so-called rebellion, he realized that there was no rebellion at all. A Zulu chief had advised his people against paying a new tax and when the British tax collector arrived, the chief killed him. The British had now set out to punish the Zulus for this crime. Gandhi sympathized with the plight of the Zulus, and he was glad that the ambulance corps had been instructed to tend their wounded. None of the white soldiers would nurse the black Zulus, most of whom were not suffering from battle injuries, but from beatings they received from abusive British soldiers.

The Zulu Rebellion made Gandhi ponder even more the principles guiding his life—truth, nonviolence, self-realization, and community service. Understanding that a commitment to these goals meant acquiring greater spiritual strength, he decided to take the vow of *brahmacharya*—control of the senses and abstinence from material and physical pleasures. Gandhi continued his experiments in education, teaching by example and shared experience. He believed that physical labor contributed to one's sense of dignity. He also stressed the learning of regional languages, which he felt increased a person's self-respect. Gandhi's own children—Harilal, Manilal, Ramdas, and Devdas—were educated according to these practices, with varying degrees of success.

Gandhi was also pledged to nonviolence, or *ahimsa*. Thoreau's term "civil disobedience" did not accurately explain Gandhi's feeling that nonviolence was a positive

PERSECUTION

Persecution is the act of subjecting people to cruel punishment because of their religion, gender, race, or beliefs.

force. "Passive resistance" implied a weakness. Gandhi's philosophy of nonviolence was based on truth and firm devotion to a just cause. He wanted Indians to name the movement, and his cousin Maganlal came up with the name that has since become the guiding principle of Gandhi's followers throughout the world. Based on *satya*—truth—and *agraha*—firmness, it is known in Gujarati as *satyagraha*. Satyagraha soon became the Indians' most effective weapon against injustice. It was, Gandhi believed, the only way to wage a moral war against persecution.

An opportunity to try satyagraha came in 1907 after the government in Transvaal passed a law which became known as the Black Act. It required Indians living in Transvaal to be fingerprinted and carry registrations cards. Taxes were also imposed, and Hindu marriages were not recognized by the state. Gandhi was outraged. He advised the Indian community to disobey the law.

At a mass meeting in Johannesburg, three thousand Indians led by Gandhi resolved to fight the new law. Various speakers addressed the crowd, which was growing more and more angry at the government and excited by the prospect of challenging it. When Gandhi got up to speak, he reminded them that if they made a pledge to refuse registration, they must accept serious risks—beatings, imprisonment, and possibly death. As

satyagrahis—or those who practice satyagraha—they would need to have extraordinary inner strength.

In January 1908, Gandhi, along with other satyagrahis, was jailed for breaking the new law. During his imprisonment he was called to a meeting with General Jan Christiaan Smuts, a leader in the Transvaal government. Smuts promised Gandhi that if Indians

Gandhi recuperates after being attacked during a protest, 1908.

registered voluntarily, the government would cancel the Act. Gandhi trusted his opponent and agreed to the compromise. However, many of his followers were mad. They felt betrayed—and when Gandhi went to register, he was brutally attacked.

Jan Christiaan Smuts

A brilliant soldier and politician, Jan Christiaan Smuts (1870-1950) was of Boer heritage but grew up under British rule. As a young man he gave up his British citizenship. By 1904, however, he decided that British and Boer cooperation was essential to the success of South Africa. Smuts was a key player in the creation of the Union of South Africa in 1910, and served twice as the country's Prime Minister.

Gandhi hurt even more when General Smuts went back on his word and the Black Act remained in force. But the Indian community was clever. They burned their registration certificates in protest and ignored a ban on immigration, which prevented them from moving from Transvaal to another state without official permission. Gandhi spent more time in jail, some of it in hard labor, but he didn't complain. He passed the days reading and praying. He felt that the real path to happiness lay in suffering for the interests of one's country and religion.

The fight against the Black Act went on for many years. Again, the government promised to do away with the law and

again it did nothing. Later, when the authorities ruled that only Christian marriages were legal in South Africa and that no more immigrants from India would be allowed to settle there, satyagraha came back in full force. Indian women were outraged that they were not considered the lawful wives of their husbands, prompting Kasturba and many other Indian women to become active in the movement. It was illegal for Indians to cross the border from Transvaal to Natal without a permit, but women from Tolstoy Farm did so anyway.

They went all the way to the town of Newcastle and persuaded Indian miners there to go on strike. For this act of disobedience, they were arrested.

Gandhi and Kasturba were both active satyagrahis.

Soon, thousands of miners marched with other Indians under Gandhi's leadership to the Transvaal border in an act of nonviolent protest. These satyagrahis were trained to be strong if confronted. They were not to fight back if stopped by force, and they were to accept any physical

and verbal abuse heaved at them. Some protestors were permanently injured and others were killed by government troops. Gandhi was arrested yet again, as were thousands of others. His goal was to fill the jails to publicize the plight of Indians in South Africa. He constantly kept the press informed of his efforts. Many expressed support for the movement. Gandhi was particularly relieved to receive some funds to support the families of poor satyagrahis who were in prison. The price of protesting was great for the many Indians who could not afford to lose weeks of wages.

Thousands of satyagrahis marched to the Transvaal border to protest the Black Act.

In 1914, Gandhi and Smuts finally came to an agreement. All Hindu and Muslim marriages would be recognized and Indians would no longer be subject to unfair taxes. Even though the immigration law would remain in effect, Gandhi was pleased with the gains satyagraha had won for his countrymen. He sent General Smuts a pair of sandals he had made while in prison. Smuts kept them for 25 years. On Gandhi's seventieth birthday, Smuts returned them with a note to his former opponent, claiming he was "not worthy to stand in the shoes of so great a man."

chapter 6

The Mahatma Returns

Gandhi decided it was time to return to India for good. He and Kasturba reached Bombay in January 1915. The inexperienced lawyer who left in a turban and suit had returned 20 years later in simple native garb. Hailed by educated Indians for his success in South Africa, he was warmly welcomed home. They called him *Mahatma,* which means "Great Soul."

Gandhi went directly to see Gopal Gokhale, his political mentor. Knowing that Gandhi was eager to practice satyagraha in India, Gokhale cautioned him to take time to reconnect with the country. Gandhi hoped to establish an ashram in Gujarat, but vowed to spend a year touring India first. Wearing clothes more typical of a laborer than a lawyer—a *dhoti* (loincloth) of Indian mill cloth and a cap—and taking only third-class transportation, the young man who was thrown from his first-class compartment in South Africa now chose to share the discomfort and inconvenience of common passengers. He witnessed the officials' contempt for his fellow travelers and realized just how much work he would have to do to change

Crowds bid farewell to the Mahatma as he leaves South Africa.

a system that allowed human beings to be treated so despicably.

During his tour, Gandhi met the Indian poet Rabindranath Tagore, who won the Nobel Prize for Literature in 1913. It may have been Tagore who first called Gandhi "Mahatma." The title would become both an honor and burden to him. He was quickly becoming seen as a savior to the Indian people. The little man was a giant in their eyes.

Rabindranath Tagore also wrote the national anthem of India.

With members from his former Phoenix Settlement, Gandhi founded the Satyagraha Ashram in Ahmedabad in May 1915. The main occupation there would be producing hand-woven cloth. The community was to be simple and self-reliant, in keeping with Gandhi's philosophy. Gandhi also believed, however, that the community should accept all who wanted to join—including untouchables. This was too much for some residents of higher castes; they could not even bear the idea of drinking water from the same well as an untouchable. But Gandhi insisted, causing the textile merchants who funded the ashram to withdraw the necessary funding. Kasturba, too, protested

When plague broke out at Satyagraha Ashram, Gandhi moved the community to this new location by the Sabarmati River. The ashram continued to make hand-woven cloth.

Gandhi's decision and threatened to leave the ashram. Finally, Gandhi got his way, and miraculously, an anonymous donor provided enough rupees to see them through another year.

In 1916, Gandhi attended a meeting of the Indian National Congress. There, a man approached him for help. The man was a poor farmer from the district of Champaran who worked on an indigo plantation, like thousands of other tenant farmers. These plantations were owned by British landlords who rented out their land. The peasants were bound by contract with these owners to grow indigo on certain portions of the land and to sell indigo to the British for a fixed price. Indigo was used to make a blue dye, but with cheaper, synthetic dyes newly available, sales of indigo had begun to decline. The landlords, therefore, passed their losses on to the tenants by increasing rent. The farmers were selling indigo at the same fixed price, but spending more to live. Not only was this unfair, but it was cruel, serving to plunge people already living in difficult

In the late 1880s, indigo was processed by hand in large vats.

circumstances into hopeless poverty. The farmers could hardly feed their families.

The next year, Gandhi went to Champaran, a small district at the foot of the Himalayas. He spoke to the secretary of the Planter's Association (which represented the landlords) on the farmers' behalf, but was told that he had no business coming between the landlords and their tenants—he was an outsider and should leave. Within a day, Gandhi was presented with a court summons. That document became his opportunity to practice civil disobedience and improve conditions.

Indigo

Vegetable dyes were used in India from about the fourth century BC. The indigo plant, *indigofera tinctoria*, was recognized as a valuable source of blue dye by early explorers to the subcontinent, including the Venetian Marco Polo, who described the indigo industry in 1298. Cultivation of the plant grew with the arrival of the Europeans in India in the 16th and 17th centuries.

Gandhi appeared before the local magistrate. He was guilty, he admitted, for not following the order to leave Champaran, but he explained, "As a law-abiding citizen my first instinct would be. . .to obey the order served upon me. But I could not do so without doing violence to my sense of duty to those for whom I have come." The charge against Gandhi was dismissed. The attention Gandhi's actions attracted embarrassed the

court. British officials at the national and state level recognized the problem and did not want to appear uncooperative with the Mahatma. They set up a committee to look into abuses in Champaran. Meanwhile, the farmers learned firsthand about the power of satyagraha. The government forced the landlords to refund a portion of rent to the farmers and the rule that said they had to grow indigo was abolished. This success showed that gains could be made by standing up for one's rights and attacking the system without violence.

Next, Gandhi was called back to Ahmedabad, where the workers in the textile mills were involved in a dispute with the owners. Wages were low and the workers had been promised a pay increase. When the promise was not fulfilled, Gandhi took up their cause. He urged the workers to carry out a peaceful strike until the bosses met their demands. The people agreed, but soon the strike became too big a burden. Without work— and pay—life was even worse than before. Gandhi sensed that this kind of civil disobedience was putting too much hardship on poor laborers. He decided to strengthen their determination by going on strike himself—a hunger strike. He pledged to fast, or refrain from eating, until the worker's demands were met. With the press covering his actions—and the country concerned for his health—the mill owners gave in. Fasting thus became an effective tool of Gandhi's satyagraha.

> **CONTROVERSIAL**
>
> Something controversial involves a difference of opinion, a dispute, or an argument.

Despite these controversial activities, Gandhi still felt

Gandhi often promoted his nonviolent campaigns in printed leaflets, such as this one dated May 6, 1919.

duty-bound to the British Empire and helped with Britain's recruiting efforts during World War I. Many Indian leaders felt differently and wanted to break with British rule. Any hopes they had for independence, however, were dashed in 1919 by passage of the Rowlatt Act. The Act threatened the basic civil rights of anyone participating in political activity against the government. Under its conditions, any person living in India could be imprisoned on suspicion of being a terrorist. Trials could be held without a jury present. Other Indian leaders joined Gandhi in opposing the Rowlatt Act—but the British became intent on implementing it.

Gandhi suggested holding a *hartal*, or strike, to protest passage of the Rowlatt Act on March 30, 1919, but postponed it until April 6, 1919. It would be a peaceful effort, with prayer and fasting. No one would work or go to school. The idea was to conduct civil disobedience on a mass scale and send a clear message to the crown and the world. But events did not unfold as Gandhi planned. Word about the postponement had not reached Delhi. A protest began peacefully there on March 30.

Police, however, grew nervous about the hartal procession and fired into the crowd, killing several people. Riots broke out in Delhi as a result. After a peaceful hartal was held in Bombay on April 6, Gandhi headed to Delhi to restore peace. He was arrested en route and taken back to Bombay. There he heard about violent acts occurring in other Indian cities and realized tensions were too great and the people too unpracticed at satyagraha to make the strike successful. He called off the hartal.

Cancellation of the hartal came too late for the city of Amritsar in the northern province of Punjab. There, in response to a number of attacks on British property, the British governor of Punjab had declared temporary rule by military authorities. Brigadier General Reginald Dyer decided to teach the natives a lesson—he took control of the city and proclaimed it unlawful to hold public meetings. On April 13, 1919, thousands of Indians—many of whom were unaware of Dyer's order—assembled in Jallianwala Bagh, the main square, to peacefully protest government oppression as well as violence against their own people. General Dyer was incensed that his authority was being challenged.

Although General Reginald Dyer had a long military career, he will forever be remembered for his role in the Amritsar Massacre.

Bullet holes pierced the walls of Jallianwala Bagh.

With armored vehicles and a column of 90 soldiers, he headed for Jallianwala Bagh.

Jallianwala Bagh is an enclosed park, bordered by buildings and walls. It has a single, narrow entrance. General Dyer's vehicles could not pass through this passage, so he marched his men in on foot. Without any warning, he ordered his men to fan out and shoot into the densely packed crowd. With no protection from the hailing bullets and no exit from the enclosure, the trapped, unarmed masses were doomed. Some dove into a well in an effort to escape the bullets and drowned. In 10 minutes, more than 1,600 bullets were fired, leaving 379 dead and 1,200 wounded. Afterwards, General Dyer would not let any Indians into the compound to help the wounded. He later said, "It was not my job. Hospitals were open and they could have gone there."

Gandhi was devastated that his call for a peaceful strike had resulted in bloodshed. He headed a commission to look into the incident. Six months later, the commission condemned

General Dyer for his actions. He was returned to England. But what happened at Amritsar changed forever the hearts of many Indians who had been loyal British subjects. The great poet Tagore renounced his knighthood, stating in a letter of protest to the viceroy on May 31, 1919: "The time has come when the badges of honour make our shame glaring in their incongruous context of humiliation, and I for my part wish to stand shorn of all special distinctions, by the side of those my countrymen who, for their so-called insignificance, are liable to suffer degradation not fit for human beings."

After the Amritsar Massacre, the British tightened their rein even more. An outraged Gandhi described the humiliation of his countrymen:

"Leaders were put under arrest, martial law, which in other words meant no law, was proclaimed.... Sentences were passed unwarranted by evidence and in flagrant violation of justice. In Amritsar innocent men and women

Avenging Amritsar: Udham Singh

Sir Michael O'Dwyer was British Lieutenant-Governor of Punjab at the time of the Amritsar Massacre. In 1940—more than 20 years after the horrifying events in Jallianwala Bagh—O'Dwyer was assassinated in London by Udham Singh, an Indian revolutionary. Singh had been in the crowd on April 13, 1919 and held O'Dwyer accountable for the bloodshed. He waited for years to seek revenge. "He was the real culprit. He deserved it. He wanted to crush the spirit of my people, so I have crushed him," he told the court. Singh was charged with the murder of Michael O'Dwyer and sentenced to death by hanging.

were made to crawl like worms on their bellies.…"

Gandhi could not support such ruthless treatment of innocent people. He could no longer be loyal to the British government. He returned the medals he had earned for his service in the Boer War and Zulu Rebellion, and he asked Indians of all religions to join him in a long hard struggle for *swaraj,* or self-rule.

This memorial in Jallianwala Bagh marks the spot of the well into which desperate protesters dove to avoid the spray of bullets fired by British troops.

Gandhi began educating people about satyagraha through two newspapers, *Young India* in English and *Navajivan* in Gujarati, and he became involved in the Indian National Congress. In 1920, he became the president of the All India Home Rule League. A formal campaign against the British began to take shape. There was to be a policy of non-cooperation in cities, towns and villages throughout the subcontinent. Gandhi was becoming even more of a hero to Indians and a much more serious threat to the viceroy.

Gandhi wrote many publications in favor of swaraj, or home rule. This is a first edition of his famous *Hind Swaraj* in English.

chapter **7**

Resistance and Reform

Events at Amritsar turned Gandhi from a social activist into a political one as well. In 1921, he became the head of the Indian National Congress. The Congress had previously been open only to Indian intellectuals. It served as a forum for those who wished to air their views about the British government and was mainly loyal to the Empire. Gandhi drafted a new constitution for the Congress. Under his direction, the Congress began to have an independent voice and reached out to all Indians—old and young, men and women, educated and unschooled. Dressed only in a hand-woven dhoti, shawl, and sandals, Gandhi traveled throughout the provinces, spreading his message of nonviolence and non-cooperation to the masses. Through non-cooperation, Gandhi hoped to weaken the British hold on Indian affairs and pressure the British Parliament to grant swaraj quickly.

Gandhi had already returned his medals of honor to the Empire. He now encouraged others who had earned similar awards to do the same. He called for government officials to stop working in

Gandhi often dressed in a khadi shawl.

the service of the Crown and for lawyers to abandon the courts. He urged students to boycott government schools and for soldiers

Two women followers of the Mahatma speak to a crowd about health and education issues.

to desert their posts. He persuaded ordinary citizens not to pay government taxes. Through his newspaper, *Young India*, and frequent speeches, his words drew support. He received delirious enthusiasm and warm affection from Punjab in the north to the tip of the peninsula. Women, who had previously played a passive role, were suddenly marching in the streets for swaraj, and thousands of poor peasants were willing to risk arrest for the cause. *Khadi*, the hand-spun and hand-woven cloth made from Indian cotton, became the uniform of Gandhi's followers. For much of its long history, India had been at the mercy of British textile mills for cloth. The textile industry was the backbone of the British

Gandhi spent part of each day spinning thread at this wheel.

economy, and the Raj unjustly required Indians to sell cotton to England. But India had its own cotton-spinning and cotton-weaving traditions. If people re-learned how to spin cotton into thread, Gandhi reasoned, they would not have to import it and the art of spinning and weaving in India would be revived. Indians could make their own cloth, keep the profits from the cotton trade, and take control of their economy. Gandhi found an old-fashioned spinning wheel and learned to spin thread from cotton fibers. He spent part of each day at the wheel, which became a symbol of self-reliance, self-respect, and the Indian independence movement.

As the spirit of non-cooperation took hold, Gandhi's followers, urged on by the Mahatma, cast their British milled clothes into bonfires. These clothes were often the only good garments

These disciples of Gandhi burn foreign clothes to protest British rule in 1922.

owned by simple villagers, but the people made this sacrifice for the promise of a free India. Yet some of the demonstrations of non-cooperation did not go as Gandhi had planned.

BOYCOTT OF FOREIGN CLOTHES

BONFIRE OF FOREIGN CLOTHES

Shall take place at the Maidan near Elphinstone Mills Opp. Elphinstone Road Station on Sunday, 31st July, 1921.

THE CEREMONY WILL BE PERFORMED BY

MAHATMA GANDHIJI

All are requested to attend in Swadeshi Clothes of Khadi. Those who have not given away their Foreign Clothes are requested to bring them to the Meeting.

SPECIAL ARRANGEMENT IS MADE FOR LADIES AND CHILDREN

IN MEMORY OF

LOKMANYA TILAK

PUBLIC MEETING AT CHAUPATI, 1st AUGUST 1921, AT 6-30 P. M.

When the Prince of Wales visited Bombay, some of Gandhi's followers attacked those who greeted the monarch. The same people who earlier heard him speak of nonviolence were storming the city in uncontrolled mobs.

This ad from the *Bombay Chronicle* instructs people to bring foreign clothes to a burning ceremony led by Gandhi.

Gandhi was horrified and sickened. He vowed to fast and observe days of silence as penance.

Gandhi decided to launch a formal non-cooperation campaign in 1922 by conducting civil disobedience in the district of Bardoli. He wanted to show the British that the people of India were determined to oppose their rule. But Gandhi's hopes were quickly brought to a halt. There was a peaceful protest march in the town of Chauri Chaura on February 5, 1922. At first, the police did not interfere and the marchers were allowed to proceed. However, some stragglers at the end of the procession got into a fight with the police. Soon there was a major struggle, and the police fired their guns into the air in an effort to disperse the crowd. When their ammunition ran out, the officers ran to the police station to take refuge from the once-passive crowd, which had lost all

73

control. The mob set fire to the station, and as the police tried to escape fiery death, they were killed. Twenty-two died.

The horror of Chauri Chaura pained Gandhi and poisoned the campaign of non-cooperation. Gandhi promptly canceled the entire effort. Upset political colleagues and disappointed followers could not understand his decision, but Gandhi believed in truth. He knew that canceling his plans might not be wise politically—it would show India's weakness to the British and severely set back the independence movement—but he believed that "it is a million times better to appear untrue before the world than to be untrue to ourselves."

News of the Mahatma's arrest on charges of sedition made the headline of the March 11, 1922 *Bombay Chronicle.*

Before the Chauri Chaura incident, the British feared arresting Gandhi for his actions against the government because it would only make his supporters more determined and create

SEDITION

Sedition is an action that provokes rebellion against a government.

chaos. But with Gandhi undergoing a five-day penance for the Chauri Chaura killings and withdrawing himself from the political fray, British

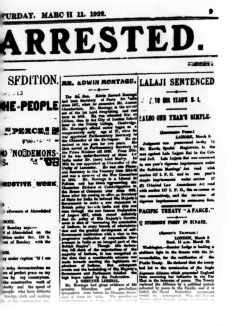

officials felt they could put him behind bars without bloodshed. He was arrested on March 10, 1922, and was charged with three counts of sedition. Gandhi pleaded guilty on all counts and told the court, "I should have known the consequences of every one of my acts. I know them. I knew that I was playing with fire. I ran the risk and if I was set free I would still do the same."

Gandhi explained to the judge that he had wanted to avoid violence, but that he had to risk fighting a system he felt was unjust, even if it meant violence might occur in the process. Still, he would respect the law and the court's judgment:

"I do not ask for mercy....I am here, therefore, to invite and cheerfully submit to the highest penalty that can be inflicted upon me for what in law is a deliberate crime, and what appears to me to be the highest duty of a citizen. The only course open to you, the judge, is . . . either to resign your post, or inflict on me the severest penalty if you believe that the system and law you are assisting to administer are good for the people."

The presiding judge addressed the Mahatma respectfully and acknowledged his status as a great spiritual leader, but he had to do his job. Gandhi was sentenced to six years in prison. The judge hoped that "if the course of events in India should make it possible for the government to reduce the period and release you, no one will be better pleased than I."

Gandhi patiently spent the many days of his prison sentence reading, praying, and spinning. The movement stalled with his disappearance from the public eye. In January 1924, he suffered acute appendicitis and was taken to a hospital for treatment. His recovery was difficult and British officials felt it would be wise to release him from the remainder of his sentence. If the

The British issued this order releasing Gandhi from prison in 1924.

Gandhi spoke at the annual session of the Muslim League, December 31, 1924.

Mahatma perished in British custody, it would surely provoke a riot.

Gandhi drinks a glass of orange juice to break his fast.

Meanwhile, politics had taken an ugly turn while Gandhi was in prison. Before launching his non-cooperation campaign years before, the Mahatma had managed to bring Muslims and Hindus together to work for independence. Both groups respected Gandhi as a holy man. In his absence, the two groups had grown apart. Religious and cultural differences that had existed for centuries became giant stumbling blocks to political harmony. Some leaders used religion as an excuse to gain political advantage. Violent skirmishes between Hindus and Muslims erupted in northern India. Gandhi saw the danger and realized that his pleas for tolerance had no effect. After days of prayer and soul-searching, he began a fast—eating no food and drinking only water—as penance for the violence. But this was no ordinary fast—it would last 21 days.

Already frail from appendicitis, Gandhi weakened rapidly and hovered near death. The newspapers and radio stations reported on his condition to an anguished nation that feared losing their beloved Bapu, or "Father," as many called him. He was well aware that the whole world was watching. Through

the great fast he hoped to teach a lesson about tolerance, even if it literally killed him. His fast had the intended result. On the twenty-first day, a unity conference was organized to discuss a peaceful resolution. Muslim and Hindu leaders joined for prayers in his presence, and the Mahatma took a sip of orange juice. The fast was over, and all was peaceful—for a while.

The Hindu-Muslim divide deeply troubled Gandhi. The National Congress was weakening as well. But after prison Gandhi needed to return to his ashram to think about the future. Ending British rule was still his goal, but India faced many other grave issues. For independence to truly be successful, the country would have to conquer poverty, poor health and hygiene, a lack of education, and a system that excluded untouchables from the community. For Gandhi, untouchability was unacceptable and not authorized by

This group portrait of women members of the Indian National Congress was taken around 1930.

the Hindu scriptures. It was a product of medieval India and actually went against Hindu traditions. He tried to educate untouchables about the way they could improve their conditions by having better hygiene and sanitary habits. The rights of women also concerned Gandhi. Kasturba actively supported Gandhi in his work, inspiring other women to work for social change and become active politically as well. There was even a British-born woman—Madeleine Slade, who Gandhi called "Mirabehn"—who became a devoted follower of the

The History of the Indian Flag

Early in the self-rule movement, a man named Pingali Venkayya came up with an idea for a national flag. Gandhi suggested adding a *charka*, or spinning wheel, as its central image, representing the economic regeneration of the Indian people. A version of this flag was used by the Indian National Congress for many years. When India's national flag was created in 1947, the spinning wheel was replaced by the *Ashoka Chakra*, representing the wheel of life.

Mahatma at this time. Gandhi strongly believed that women could play an important role in the country's struggle.

So, for the next few years, Gandhi worked toward reform and promoted the khadi movement. He kept a religious vow of observing silence and fasting on Mondays. All the while, Hindus and Muslims struggled to live in peace, but political ambitions seemed determined to keep them apart.

chapter **8**

Salt and Sweat

The Simon Commission arrived in India in 1928, with the task of reviewing the workings of Britain's Indian government and reporting recommendations for India's future. The Indians were deeply insulted. No Indians were asked to be on the commission, despite promises that Indians would participate in the government of their own country. The message from Britain was loud and clear: We will continue to make the rules regardless of India's wishes.

Although many political parties were united in their distrust of the Simon Commission, there was still a good deal of disagreement about self-rule between the Hindu majority and the Muslim minority. Gandhi seemed to be the only figure who could bridge the gap between them. With his guidance, the Congress issued a declaration of independence on January 26, 1930. Unlike the American Declaration of Independence, the hope was to wage a war against the Empire with satyagraha

Trained to confront their adversary lying down, these satyagrahis participate in a nonviolent protest.

instead of swords and guns. Gandhi felt that a new satyagraha effort was essential to show the British that khadi-wearing Indians who spun their own cloth were in charge of their own destiny. But he needed to find a focus for the new campaign. Gandhi listed 11 points on which reform was needed, but the one he chose to dramatize had great meaning for Indians: the tax on salt.

GANDHIJI'S TEN COMMANDMENTS

"PERSONALLY, I WOULDN'T MAKE MUCH HEADWAY WITH 'EM IN MY BUSINESS. THEY ARE TOO IMPRACTICAL FOR MODERN CONDITIONS. BUT, OH BOY! WHAT A CLEAN-UP I COULD MAKE IF I HAD THE CONFIDENCE OF MILLIONS OF PEOPLE, THE WAY HE HAS!"

"THEY'RE ALL RIGHT FOR PLANKS IN A PLATFORM BUT NOT FOR PRACTICAL, EVERY DAY POLITICAL USE."

PROMOTER

POLITICIAN

GANDHI'S PERSONAL TEN COMMANDMENTS FOR HIS OWN GUIDANCE—

1. Truth.
2. Love.
3. Chastity.
4. Restraint of the Appetites.
5. Possession only of essentials.
6. One's Bread must be earned by the Sweat of one's brow.
Man's duty is to serve his neighbor.
Equality of Mankind.
Equality of all the Great Faiths of the World.
Fearlessness

The characters in this cartoon mock Gandhi's personal philosophy, which some people felt was impractical in the modern world.

Ever since the time of the East India Company, British law had stated that the sale and production of salt by anyone other than the British was a criminal offense. This ruling allowed the Raj to tax salt and earn a large profit because salt was a basic necessity. Although the actual amount of the tax was quite small, its symbolism was great. The fact that Britain had complete control over a natural resource of India was something all Indians—whether professors or peasants—could rally against. Gandhi wrote a letter to Lord Irwin, viceroy of India, proclaiming the tax evil

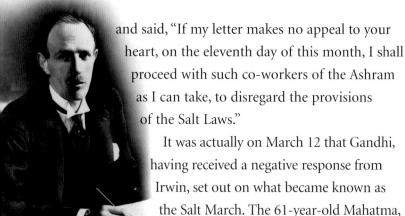

and said, "If my letter makes no appeal to your heart, on the eleventh day of this month, I shall proceed with such co-workers of the Ashram as I can take, to disregard the provisions of the Salt Laws."

It was actually on March 12 that Gandhi, having received a negative response from Irwin, set out on what became known as the Salt March. The 61-year-old Mahatma, accompanied by 78 of his most trusted volunteers—carefully picked to represent Hindus, Muslims, and other diverse groups of India—left Satyagraha Ashram on foot. His goal was to walk to Dandi, 240 miles (386 kilometers) away on the Gujarat coast. He walked briskly and happily. In the scorching sun, he managed to cover 10 miles (16 kilometers) a day, stopping to

Lord Irwin was not moved by Gandhi's concerns about the salt tax.

Mahatma Gandhi walks with his followers on the Salt March.

rest in villages, where he was greeted warmly. Gandhi educated young Indians in these villages about satyagraha, and many were encouraged to join the march. Soon they were a thousand strong.

Indian women openly defy British law by filling brass pots with saltwater, which, when evaporated, yields pure salt.

Although many in the Indian Congress were still unsure of the meaning of the protest, by the third week the march had generated interest worldwide. Newspapers and radio stations were following the story closely—with the press walking alongside the satyagrahis. On the evening of April 5, the weary marchers reached the coast and spent that night in prayer. At dawn on April 6, Gandhi bathed in the sea as a symbol of purification. On his way back to the beach, he bent down and picked up some salt brought in by the tide. With that simple act, Gandhi had broken the law.

The reporters rushed to send their dispatches. Word of Gandhi's action was out across India—and on its way to the world. Within days, thousands of Indians were lining the coastlines of India and breaking the law. Congress president

Jawaharlal Nehru was ashamed that he had doubted Gandhi. The Mahatma had a genius for understanding the people of his country. Their enthusiasm for breaking unjust laws seemed unlimited. Indians were illegally making and selling salt in country markets and on city streets. In some places, British shops were picketed and goods were boycotted. The British put about 50,000 people in jail. Their patience was wearing thin.

On May 4, around midnight, Gandhi was awakened by the police, arrested, and taken to Yeravda Jail. Gandhi and his followers embraced the prison experience with courage. The viceroy wanted no trial, which would only give Gandhi the opportunity to arouse the passions of his supporters. He wanted him quietly behind bars and the court had the power to keep him there.

But the viceroy had underestimated the satyagrahis, who were now better trained and more disciplined than they had been when violence occurred in Chauri Chaura. On May 21, one of Gandhi's disciples, a woman named Sarojini Naidu,

A native policeman armed with a *lathi* (bamboo stick bound in iron) fights off a mob at the salt works in Wadala.

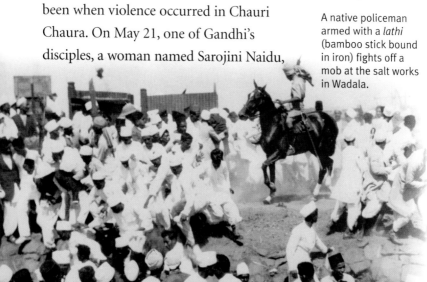

led 2,500 volunteers to attempt a raid of the government's Dharasana Salt Works. The Works were guarded by a few hundred Indian police under British command. Webb Miller, a United Press reporter, wrote:

Sarojini Naidu, who appeared on the cover of this French magazine in 1930, was jailed for her actions in the salt protests.

"In complete silence the Gandhi men drew up and halted a hundred yards from the stockade. A picked column advanced from the crowd, waded the ditches, and approached the barbed-wire….Suddenly, at a word of command, scores of native policemen rushed upon the marchers and rained blows on their heads with their steel-shod lathis. Not one of the marchers even raised an arm to fend off the blows.… From where I stood I heard the sickening whack of the clubs on unprotected skulls.…The survivors, without breaking ranks, silently and doggedly marched on until struck down."

Miller counted 320 wounded and 2 dead. Sarojini Naidu was arrested and sent to prison. But the satyagrahis had confronted the troops in a passive, dignified manner. Satyagraha had triumphed. The rest of the world read about the British brutality with disgust. Britain was losing its grip on India.

In the meantime, Lord Irwin was becoming frustrated. He was an oppressor—a role he didn't want or like. He was also upset by the outcome of the First Round Table Conference, held in England in 1930 to discuss the future of India. Although there were many Indian delegates there, no members of the Indian National Congress were invited, and little real progress was made. Later, the British realized they would have to work with the Congress, since it was India's most prominent party. As a gesture toward cooperation, Lord Irwin released Gandhi and other Congress members from prison.

Gandhi and Irwin signed a pact in New Delhi on March 5, 1931. Gandhi agreed to call off the civil disobedience campaign and the boycotts of British goods. Irwin agreed to release all political prisoners and allow the poor along the coast to make and collect salt locally for home consumption. Now Gandhi appealed to the people to maintain the discipline they had shown during non-cooperation. He did not want violence to ruin the progress earned through the Salt March. Gandhi could sense that negotiations with Lord Irwin were a gain for India, even if not a complete victory. He looked

In sandals and khadi shawl, Gandhi arrives in Folkstone, England, in a sea of formal dressers, on September 12, 1931.

forward to making further steps toward swaraj at the Second Round Table Conference in London.

Gandhi arrived at the conference in September of 1931. Years before, he had arrived in London in an inappropriate white suit, and now his appearance was just as odd—but in a dhoti and shawl he was totally comfortable.

Women textile workers in Lancashire greet their foreign visitor.

After a visit to Buckingham Palace, he was asked if he felt underdressed in relation to King George V. Gandhi joked, "The King had on enough for both of us."

Gandhi found a house in one of the poorest sections of London, where he could meet the locals. He even visited Lancashire, where mill workers who had lost work because of his khadi program showered him with affection. Although his political campaign had cost them personal hardship, they appreciated his commitment to workers and the poor.

The conference itself did not work out as Gandhi had hoped. Britain's new conservative government seemed uninterested in India's independence, and the Indian delegation could not agree on the balance of power between Hindus and Muslims and the status of untouchables in the future government. India had a lot more work to do before achieving self-rule.

Gandhi returned to India in December 1931 only to find that he was not welcome at home. In his absence, the new viceroy, Lord Willingdon—who had recently taken Lord Irwin's place—had enacted harsh repressive measures and some provinces were under virtual martial law. Gandhi appealed to Lord Willingdon to speak with him in person about the situation, but Willingdon would not see him. Gandhi felt that the pact he had made with Lord Irwin had been broken. He and the Congress launched a new phase of civil disobedience.

Lord Willingdon, the viceroy who once referred to Gandhi as "clever as a barrel load of monkeys," could not suppress the satyagraha movement.

The next day, on January 4, 1932, Gandhi was put in prison. Other members of the Congress were also arrested. In the first two months of 1932, 35,000 people were hauled off to jail. In his cell in Yeravda Prison, Gandhi was restricted but not powerless. When he read in a newspaper about a British proposal stating that the new government of India should have a certain number of representatives for untouchables, elected only by untouchables, he was upset. He felt that untouchables should not be treated as separate from all other Hindus

This scene shows Gandhi's 1932 arrest for acts of civil disobedience.

and that swaraj would never be achieved unless the Hindu hatred of untouchables was healed. From his cell, he sent a letter to the British government protesting the creation of this electorate and vowed to fast to the death to oppose it. He stopped eating on September 20, 1932. Many were outraged that Gandhi would fast to influence a political outcome. This went beyond fasting as penance. But Gandhi knew that the discrimination toward untouchables was deeply rooted.

By the end of the first week of the fast, Gandhi was too weak to walk. Frantic negotiations were going on between Hindu leaders and the British government. All were concerned that Gandhi would die. Meanwhile, the world was opening—as if by magic—to untouchables. They were suddenly allowed to draw water at public wells and enter upper-caste temples to worship. On September 26, the British approved a plan allowing untouchables to vote with Hindus in joint elections. Gandhi took a sip of orange juice and broke the fast. The two nations—Britain and India—breathed a sigh of relief.

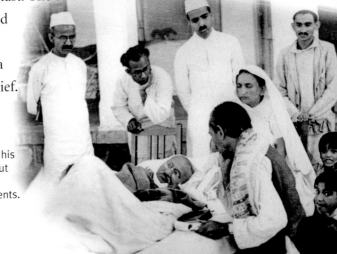

Gandhi's fasts provoked concern among his followers and put pressure on his political opponents.

chapter **9**

Independence for India

Gandhi's great fast had offered some hope to untouchables, but he realized that there was more work to do. After his release from prison, Gandhi devoted all his time to working on behalf of this depressed class. He founded a newspaper called *Harijan,* or "Children of God," which was the term he used for the untouchables. It asked upper-caste Hindus to change their attitudes toward these impoverished people. Gandhi also embarked on a trip throughout India to deliver his message in person. However, Gandhi's ideas were not always popular with Hindus who were bound to the ancient caste system. In 1934, he was on his way to give a speech when a bomb was thrown at the cars in his party. Fortunately, the car he was in was spared. The Mahatma would not give up. He continued to do his work.

Gandhi retired from the Indian National Congress in

As at Wardha
C.P.
India.
23.7.'39.

Dear friend,

Friends have been urging me to write to you for the sake of humanity. But I have resisted their request, because of the feeling that any letter from me would be an impertinence. Something tells me that I must not calculate and that I must make my appeal for whatever it may be worth.

It is quite clear that you are today the one person in the world who can prevent a war which may reduce humanity to the savage state. Must you pay that price for an object however worthy it may appear to you to be ? Will you listen to the appeal of one who has deliberately shunned the method of war not without considerable success? Any way I anticipate your forgiveness, if I have erred in writing to you.

I remain,
Your sincere friend
M.K.Gandhi

Herr Hitler
Berlin
Germany.

Gandhi wrote to Adolf Hitler, begging him to prevent the outbreak of world war.

1934, although he kept in close touch with its influential leaders Vallabhbhai Patel and Jawaharlal Nehru. By the late 1930s, he was living at Sevagram Ashram in Wardhi. Although he was still focused on events in his country, he was well aware that a political storm was brewing in Germany with the rise of Nazi leader Adolf Hitler. Hitler's plans to conquer France and Britain were apparent. Gandhi, firmly believing that violence never solved anything, wrote a letter to the dictator: "It is quite clear that you are today the one person in the world who can prevent a war which may reduce humanity to the savage state."

Gandhi was distraught about Hitler's persecution of the Jews. He wrote, "If there ever could be a justifiable war in the name of and for humanity, war against Germany would be completely justified." But Gandhi continued to insist that despite Hitler's evil government, "I do not believe in any war." Some of his ideas were deeply troubling to those most threatened by tyranny. He suggested that Jews practice satyagraha and that the British let Hitler take their island

Adolf Hitler (1889–1945)

Adolf Hitler became Chancellor of Germany in 1933 and Führer (Leader) of Germany in 1934. He was also the head of the Nazi Party. Hitler reached the height of his power during World War II, when his armies dominated Europe. His racist policies resulted in the death of more than six million people, a genocide known as the Holocaust. Hitler committed suicide in 1945.

rather than fight. He didn't seem to grasp the German dictator's frightening intentions.

When the British went to war, they took India into the fray with them, without consulting the Indian National Congress. Gandhi opposed India's involvement in the war at all costs. But his Congress colleagues, particularly Nehru, thought gains might be made toward Indian independence if they cooperated. Nehru was also worried about the Japanese, who, like Germany, had imperialist plans, and were much closer to India's borders. India might need Britain's help to fight off Japan if it attacked. The Congress wanted to make a deal: we'll fight for you, and you grant us independence. Prime Minister Winston Churchill would not hear of it: "I have not become the King's First Minister in order to preside at the liquidation of the British Empire," he declared.

With the Japanese threat growing stronger, and international pressure increasing, Churchill decided to send a representative to India to

Jawaharlal Nehru and Sir Stafford Cripps discuss the possibility of giving India Dominion status in 1942.

make an offer. Sir Stafford
Cripps arrived in India on
March 22, 1942. A member
of Churchill's war cabinet,
he was a personal friend of
Nehru and sympathized with
the Indian cause. Cripps
carried a proposal to the
Congress: In exchange for India's
all-out participation in the war,
India could have Dominion status—
similar to Canada's arrangement with
Britain—when the war ended. In addition,

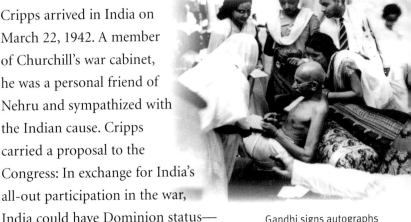

Gandhi signs autographs
at the All–India Congress
in Bombay in 1942.

India's provinces, princely states, and minorities could, if
they desired, have separate settlement agreements with
the British. After the war, these individual territories could
withdraw from the British Commonwealth if they wished.

Cripps's proposal was unacceptable to Gandhi and the
Congress. If his plan was put into effect, India could be
split into many parts. Each state could have a separate
government and act like a separate country. The Congress
could not accept an offer that left India fragmented and
weak. In any event, Gandhi still opposed the war and
would not approve of India's involvement in it. There
was not going to be any deal. Cripps returned to Britain
empty-handed, and Gandhi made new plans to free
India from British rule.

The civil-disobedience movement had been put on hold during Gandhi's travels and work on behalf of the untouchables, but the Cripps proposal convinced Gandhi that India needed full independence, and that they had to demand it now. Before beginning a new campaign, Gandhi sent his special assistant, the British-born Mirabehn, with a message for Lord Linlithgow, the current viceroy. But Linlithgow would not reply. So Gandhi's new protest was launched on August 8, 1942. With words as sharp as weapons, Gandhi said, "I want freedom immediately, this very night, before dawn, if it can be had." He asked followers to "do or die" for India and pledged: "We shall not live to see the perpetuation of our slavery." The slogan of the campaign was "Quit India!" The British took this as a

Although Gandhi changed the focus of his campaigns, he continued to care deeply about India's underprivileged class, which struggles with poverty long after the Mahatma's death.

threat and Gandhi, along with some Congress leaders, was immediately arrested.

Gandhi's arrest unleashed a storm of violence against the British. Indians took to the streets, attacking government buildings and British citizens. Lord Linlithgow blamed Gandhi for the unrest, insisting that his words had whipped the masses into a frenzy. But Gandhi believed it was his arrest by the British government that had caused such backlash. Gandhi was 73 years old—small and frail, but with a firm faith in God. He decided to begin another fast to end the violence and

Mirabehn

Madeleine Slade, or Mirabehn, was the daughter of a British admiral, and spent part of her childhood in Bombay. Years later, after reading a book about Gandhi, she gave up her family connections. Trading European dresses for a sari of khadi, she devoted her life to the Mahatma, living at his ashrams and following him to prison. Mirabehn became a daring foot soldier in the satyagraha movement and assisted Gandhi in his various campaigns to achieve independence for India.

the feud with the viceroy. Back in England, Prime Minister Churchill had had enough of Gandhi's strange tactics. He instructed the viceroy to "let the little man starve if need be." However, other British officials knew there would be terrible consequences if Gandhi died in prison.

Gandhi did not mind being in prison. He had his long-time secretary, Mahadev Desai, with him, as well as Kasturba,

who had been arrested for carrying on Gandhi's work after he was taken into custody. Desai had been Gandhi's right-hand man for more than 20 years. The Mahatma trusted Desai and discussed all his day-to-day decisions with him. A pleasant, scholarly man who often seemed to read the Mahatma's mind, he accompanied Gandhi to all his meetings and kept the press informed of the Mahatma's thoughts and deeds. So it was an enormous blow when, just days after their imprisonment, Desai died suddenly of a heart attack.

Gandhi was reeling from the loss of Desai when Kasturba's health began to decline. At the age of 74, she was slowing down. Locked in prison, she missed the community of the ashram. Gandhi spent time caring for his wife and taking walks with her around the prison grounds, but she continued to deteriorate. She came down with pneumonia and eventually developed acute bronchitis. As her condition worsened, doctors were flown in to treat her with injections of penicillin. Gandhi, however, prevented the doctors from giving her

Mahadev Desai was a young lawyer when he decided to join Gandhi's movement. He was the Mahatma's devoted secretary for more than 25 years, from 1917 to 1942. Desai wrote several books about Gandhi.

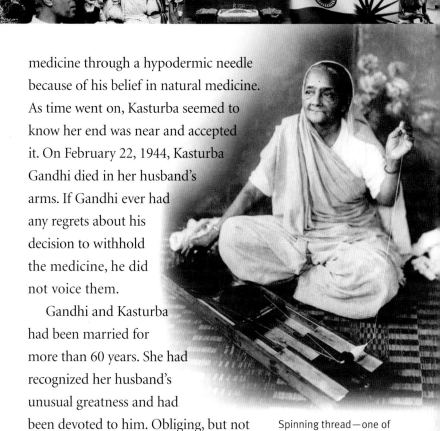

medicine through a hypodermic needle because of his belief in natural medicine. As time went on, Kasturba seemed to know her end was near and accepted it. On February 22, 1944, Kasturba Gandhi died in her husband's arms. If Gandhi ever had any regrets about his decision to withhold the medicine, he did not voice them.

Gandhi and Kasturba had been married for more than 60 years. She had recognized her husband's unusual greatness and had been devoted to him. Obliging, but not meek, she had adapted gracefully to a demanding life. The Mahatma seemed

Spinning thread—one of the many ways Kasturba supported Gandhi's work.

a lost soul without her. Mirabehn noted that it was as if a part of him departed. After Kasturba's death, Gandhi's own health started to fail, and British authorities grew concerned that he would die in prison. He was released on May 6, 1944, from his final term as a British prisoner. In total, Gandhi had been jailed for 2,089 days in India and 249 days in South Africa. For several months he was not able to return to work, but by the autumn of 1944 he found the strength to move on.

Despite Gandhi's appeals, Jinnah insisted on having a Muslim state.

When Gandhi went back to work he also began a correspondence with the new viceroy, Lord Wavell. But immediate independence for India was not a topic the British cared to discuss in the midst of a war. A serious issue also faced Hindus and Muslims before an agreement with Britain could be reached: unity. The Muslim League, led by Mohammed Ali Jinnah, was concerned that the Hindu majority would take over an independent India.

Gandhi tried to reach out to Jinnah, who, like himself, had been educated in England and was an attorney. But while Gandhi had simplified his life and given up possessions, Jinnah was more than comfortable with his wealth. While Gandhi traveled in third-class compartments, Jinnah rode first class and stayed in luxurious European-style hotels. Although many saw Jinnah as only interested in politics and power, others saw him as a staunch advocate for the Muslim minority. Gandhi tried to persuade him that religious unity was essential for national unity, but Jinnah felt that religious unity would kill the dream of a Muslim nation. He wanted a separate state for Muslims. It would be called Pakistan, and he would be its ruler.

Jinnah had not always held such views. Years before, he had been a Gandhi supporter, working for Hindu-Muslim unity along with independence, but Jinnah disliked Gandhi's civil-disobedience campaigns. He could not understand Gandhi's affection for the poor. He wanted a nation run by the educated upper class, not the illiterate masses. He could not understand Gandhi's approach, and Gandhi could not accept his.

In 1945, Clement Atlee replaced Winston Churchill as Britain's prime minister. Atlee's party favored self-rule for India, but Atlee quickly realized that a solution to the Hindu-Muslim problem had to be found soon or there would be terrible bloodshed between the groups. He was right. Riots broke out in Calcutta in the summer of 1946. That fall, Hindus and Muslims engaged in brutal attacks on each other in the Noakhali and Bihar regions. The murders were so frequent and barbaric in some places that blood literally ran in the streets. Gandhi's pleas for nonviolence were not heeded.

Policemen in Calcutta use tear gas to break up riots.

Clement Atlee knew just the man to help India achieve independence. Ironically, that man was the great-grandson of Queen Victoria, the first Empress of India. Louis Mountbatten was a World War II war hero who had visited India back in the 1920s when traveling with the Prince of Wales. During his stay, he had attended lavish parties and polo matches, ridden on elephants, and hunted tigers. He had also met Edwina, the lovely woman who was to become his bride.

Mountbatten was not eager to take the job of viceroy when Atlee offered it to him. He knew that helping India achieve independence was an enormous challenge, one that might tarnish his brilliant naval

The Mahatma meets with weeping women after the outbreak of riots between Hindus and Muslims in Bengal, 1946.

career. So, he set a condition. He would accept the position of India's last viceroy, but a definite date for the British to grant independence had to be established. Mountbatten arrived in India on March 22, 1947. The date for India to become a self-ruling nation was set for August 15.

Mountbatten had his work cut out for him. The tall, handsome son of the Empire met with the little Mahatma, as well as with Nehru, Patel, and Jinnah. Determined to bring the leaders together, he labored to forge a personal bond with each and win his confidence. He was largely successful—except with Jinnah. Jinnah threatened that the Muslims would destroy India if they could not have a separate Pakistan. With no other course—and no more time—Mountbatten gave in. Nehru, Patel, and other leaders of the Congress reluctantly followed suit. Independence for two countries was better than no independence at all. India would be free—but divided.

Lord Mountbatten (1900–1976)

Louis Mountbatten was related to both British and German royalty. He was a naval commander early in World War II, and became Supreme Commander of the Allied Forces in South East Asia in 1943. As viceroy of India, Mountbatten struggled to preserve India as a single country. Criticized by some for the breakup of India because of his rigid timetable for independence, he was praised by others for having resolved matters quickly and justly.

chapter 10

Division and Death

Gandhi once said, "You'll have to divide my body before you divide India." As August 1947 approached it seemed that if his body didn't break, his heart would. He had devoted his life to nonviolence and to bringing his countrymen together in an independent India, but as the day that was to have been a triumph drew closer, horrible violence broke out.

Dividing India into two was very complicated because Hindus, Muslims, and other religious groups had lived together—mostly in harmony, sometimes not—in the towns, small villages, and cities of the subcontinent for centuries. Now Muslims had to decide if they would leave India for Pakistan. Hindus in the area that would become Pakistan had the same problem: Should they stay or leave? The way in which India and Pakistan were to be carved up made matters even more difficult. Punjab would now be partly in India and partly in Pakistan. Even Pakistan

We deeply deplore the recent acts of lawlessness and violence that have brought the utmost disgrace on the fair name of India and the greatest misery to innocent people, irrespective of who were the aggressors and who were the victims.

We denounce for all time the use of force to achieve political ends, and we call upon all the communities of India, to whatever persuasion they may belong, not only to refrain from all acts of violence and disorder; but also to avoid both in speech and writing, any words which might be construed as an incitement to such acts.

M. A. Jinnah
15/4/47
c.e. Mohandas

Gandhi and Jinnah released this joint appeal for peace among different religious groups.

itself was divided—into West Pakistan and East Pakistan, which later became Bangladesh.

The country was in an uproar; violence had broken out in Punjab and Bengal. In an effort to stop the bloodshed, Gandhi traveled through India. He headed to Noakhali district in Bengal, where the Muslim League was in power. There, many Hindus had been victims of murder and forced conversions. He went to bring peace and was willing to risk his life to do so. In Noakhali, the 77-year-old Hindu walked through rough terrain from village to village, dressed in khadi and eating only fruit and nuts. He was determined to mend the conflict between Hindus and Muslims. Then he traveled to Bihar, a Hindu area, and collected money for injured and homeless Muslims, who had suffered greatly at the hands of the Hindus, to set an example of love and compassion. This time his efforts didn't seem to be enough—and the day for independence was just months away.

The Mahatma walks alone in Noakhali, Bengal, in 1946.

At the stroke of midnight on August 15, 1947, the ancient land of the Moguls was divided into two nations—India and Pakistan. Gandhi had long anticipated the moment when the

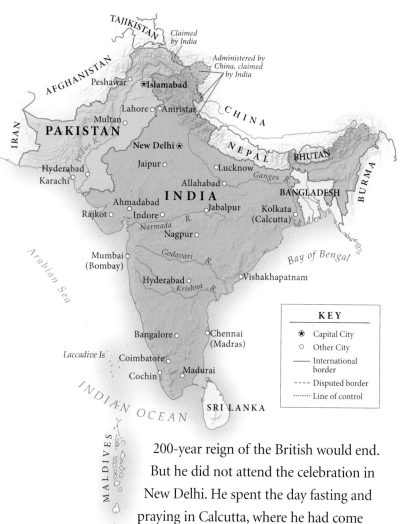

200-year reign of the British would end. But he did not attend the celebration in New Delhi. He spent the day fasting and praying in Calcutta, where he had come to keep the peace in the hectic days before independence. Gandhi's presence still had a magical effect on Indians of all religions and castes. On the eve of the celebration, he cautioned his countrymen: "If the flames of communal strife

envelop the whole country, how can our newborn freedom survive?" The crowds cheered him, but Gandhi was not happy.

The union between Hindus and Muslims in Calcutta was fragile and broke apart in a burst of violence on August 31. As he had done so effectively in the past, Gandhi began a fast. The looting, murder, and arson came to a halt. The city's religious leaders met with Gandhi and signed a pledge to maintain control. But Calcutta was only one city.

In Punjab, where the partition of Pakistan and India was a physical reality

Jawaharlal Nehru (1889-1964)

Jawaharlal Nehru was Gandhi's trusted lieutenant in the satyagraha movement. For his participation in Gandhi's campaigns he served several prison terms, totaling nine years in all. Nehru was president of the Indian National Congress and became, at age 57, independent India's first prime minister. His daughter, Indira, and grandson, Rajiv, also served as prime ministers of India.

as well as an emotional one, there was hysteria. Hindus were leaving Pakistan in droves and Muslims were streaming in from the Indian border. Massacres of Hindus and Muslims were an almost daily occurrence. Train cars carrying refugees were often attacked by angry mobs, and pulled into railroad stations full of corpses—no one was left alive. Barbaric acts against Hindus and Sikhs in West Pakistan were matched

by ghastly attacks on Muslims. The government seemed powerless to control the tragedy. Between 1946 and 1947 more than 5,000 people had been killed. After independence, the number grew into the hundreds of thousands. The 78-year-old founder of the satyagraha movement watched with "nothing but anguish in [his] heart."

Gandhi decided to go see for himself what was happening in Punjab. His train stopped first in Delhi, where he was told that rioting and looting was out of control. He was forced to stay in Delhi rather than continue on to Punjab. There, he served on the Emergency Committee established by Mountbatten and Nehru. Gandhi had always been a spiritual leader for both Hindus and Muslims, but in Delhi he encountered anger from his former supporters. Hindus were angry that he would show sympathy toward Muslims. Muslims saw him as the enemy because he was Hindu. The Mahatma felt helpless. It was time to see what God had to say. Gandhi began another fast on January 13, 1948.

Now an old man, Gandhi's decline was rapid. He fell in and out of consciousness. On January 18, after five very difficult days, political and religious leaders came to assure Gandhi that attacks on Muslims by Hindus and on Hindus by Muslims would end. Satisfied by their solemn pledge, Gandhi broke his fast. Leaders sighed with relief. Prayers were said.

EXTREMIST

An extremist is a person who advocates actions or policies considered to be uncompromising or extreme.

Many thought that if the Mahatma had not forced the issue through his selfless act, civil war would have erupted and destroyed both India and Pakistan.

After the fast, the unrest and anger that prompted it did not truly go away. Hindu extremists were outraged by Gandhi's tactics. They felt he was manipulating Hindus to please Muslims for political reasons. They believed that his sympathy with Muslims in India and Pakistan compromised the safety and rights of the Hindu majority. Two days after the fast ended, Gandhi's evening prayer—a public event— was disrupted by a bomb. Gandhi wasn't hurt in the blast, and he wasn't concerned. Some thought Gandhi should have police protection,

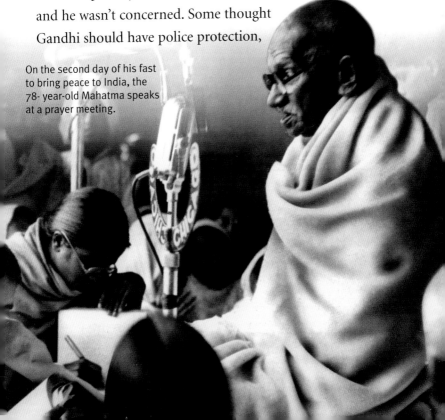

On the second day of his fast to bring peace to India, the 78- year-old Mahatma speaks at a prayer meeting.

but the Mahatma believed "to die by the hand of a brother… cannot be for me a matter of sorrow."

Gandhi was still weak from his fast on January 30, but he hurried to his evening prayer meeting. He hated to be late. Supported on each side by his grandnieces Manubehn and Abhabehn, he entered the large garden at Birla House where an expectant crowd awaited him. Gandhi raised his hands, palms clasped together to greet his supporters. Many tried to come forward to touch the feet of the man they worshipped, but one man forced himself past the others. As he kneeled before the Mahatma, he aimed a semi automatic pistol at Gandhi's heart and pulled the trigger. Uttering *"He Ram"* ("Oh God"), Gandhi fell back. His khadi was stained with blood, he slumped to the ground and his heart stopped beating. His face was at peace.

Gandhi's assassin was caught after a brief struggle. His name was Nathuram Godse. Godse was a member of a Hindu extremist group that felt betrayed by Gandhi because he showed support to Muslims. Others had helped Godse plan the Mahatma's

Gandhi's death made newspaper headlines across the world. Here it is announced on the front page of Calcutta's *Hindusthan Standard*.

murder. Godse and one of his co-conspirators were later tried, convicted, and executed for the crime.

For Jawaharlal Nehru, who had now become prime minister of India, Gandhi had been almost a father. His voice breaking with emotion, he addressed his new and troubled nation on the radio after he learned the sad news of the Mahatma's death:

"The light has gone out of our lives and there is darkness everywhere and I do not quite know what to tell you and how to say it. Our beloved leader, Bapu as we called him, the father of our nation, is no more....The light has gone out, I said, and yet I was wrong. For the light that shone in this country was no ordinary light. The light that has illumined this country for these many years, and the world will see it and it will give solace to innumerable hearts. For that light represented the living truth, and the eternal man was with us with his eternal

The men accused of assassinating Gandhi appear in a New Delhi courtroom. Nathuram Godse is front center.

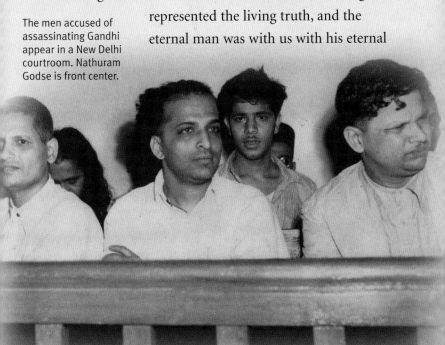

truth reminding us of the right path, drawing us from error, taking this ancient country to freedom...."

Ed Snow, a journalist who had known Gandhi personally, was in Delhi in 1948. Several months after Gandhi died, he wrote this moving recollection of Gandhi's death:

"What I remember about...the night Gandhi was killed was how much more terrible a moment it was than anyone can describe in words. Men and women did not really grieve...for Gandhi, who died almost instantly.... But each man mourned for something in himself left without a friend, a personal sorrow, as if fate had

Gandhi's body takes its final journey through a sea of mourners.

seized an intimate treasure
that one always assumed
would be there....

This small man, so full of
a large love of men, extended
beyond India and beyond
time....There was a mirror
in the Mahatma in which
everyone could see the best in
himself, and when the mirror
broke, it seemed...the thing in
oneself might be fled forever."

In Hindu tradition,
Gandhi's body was cremated.
His funeral pyre was lit at
Raj Ghat on the banks of the
River Jamuna on January 31.
His funeral drew more than
one million people—one of
the biggest crowds in history.

Hindu Cremation

Hindus cremate, or burn, the
dead to release the soul from
its earthly existence. If the body
is not cremated, it is believed
that the soul remains nearby for
days or months. The standard
cremation ceremony begins with
the ritual cleansing, dressing, and
adorning of the body. The body
is then carried to the cremation
ground as prayers are chanted.
It is the chief mourner, usually
the eldest son, who lights the
pyre on which the body rests,
offering the dead to heaven.

Ironically, the funeral procession was organized as a military
operation by Lord Mountbatten, who still served as the
commander-in-chief of India's army. The Mahatma's body
went on its last journey in an army vehicle. The man who
preached nonviolence had a funeral carriage drawn by units
of India's army, navy, and air force. Military bombers flew
overhead and dipped low in salute.

chapter 11

Gandhi's Truth

Gandhi's message of truth continues to inspire and motivate people of all generations and in all regions of the world. Although India and Pakistan maintain only a fragile peace today, both countries were the beneficiaries of Gandhi's quest for freedom. His work to lift the untouchables from a life of squalor and shame bore fruit in India and served as an inspiration to oppressed classes throughout the world—from African-Americans in America's segregated South to black South Africans living under apartheid. His appeal to people of all races and religions to lead a moral, truthful life has echoed far beyond the shores of India.

Gandhi was not afraid to ask difficult questions and experiment with possible solutions. This openness of mind allowed him to reach millions in a huge country plagued by poverty and oppression, separated by faith and tradition, and dominated by a difficult landscape. For Gandhi, India's political problems had a very human face. He asked his fellow men to "recall the face of the poorest and

> *"Mahatma Gandhi will go down in history on a par with Buddha and Jesus Christ."*
>
> –Lord Mountbatten, the last British viceroy of India

most helpless man you have ever seen and ask yourself if the step you contemplate is going to be of any use to him….Will it restore to him control over his own life and destiny? In other words, will it lead to…self-rule for the hungry and spiritually starved millions of our countrymen? Then you will find your doubts and your self melting away."

Martin Luther King, Jr., the prominent U.S. civil-rights leader of the 1950s and 1960s, was introduced to Gandhi's teachings while studying to be a minister. The young man was captivated by the philosophy of nonviolent resistance. He saw that Gandhi's radical techniques had brought about

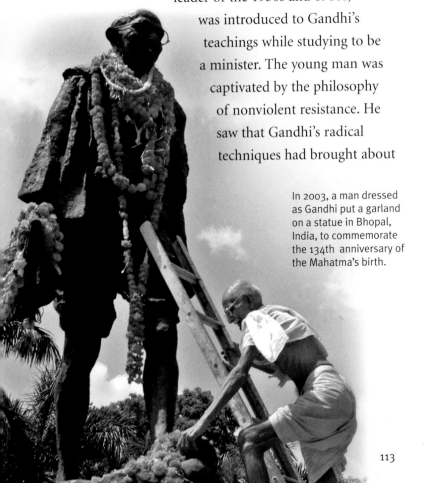

In 2003, a man dressed as Gandhi put a garland on a statue in Bhopal, India, to commemorate the 134th anniversary of the Mahatma's birth.

113

great social change in India and wondered if those same techniques would work in his own country.

King was impressed that Gandhi had learned to free himself from the hatred of his oppressors. As a black boy growing up in the segregated South, King had felt the bitterness caused by racism and had understood his people's rage toward the white community. But Gandhi thought that if you freed yourself from rage, you could accomplish good for all mankind. Gandhi took Jesus's message of "love your enemy" to a new level.

Though King did not call his campaign satyagraha, he employed Gandhi's nonviolent methods during the Montgomery bus boycott of 1955–1956. The boycott began when Rosa Parks, a black woman, broke an Alabama law by refusing to give up her bus seat to a white passenger. This act, similar to the khadi movement, hurt business and disrupted life in Montgomery, finally pressuring local officials to resolve the crisis and forcing the courts to change an unjust law. Like the indigo farmers in Champaran, India, the people of Montgomery saw the positive power of nonviolent resistance.

Martin Luther King, Jr., leads a nonviolent march for civil rights in Selma, Alabama, 1965.

King visited India in 1959. Seeing the horrible conditions imposed on untouchables by the caste system—a system Gandhi opposed—he felt that the plight of African-Americans was similar. The trip confirmed for King what he already knew: He must walk in Gandhi's footsteps.

Like Gandhi and Martin Luther King, Jr., Nelson Mandela of South Africa became a leader because of extraordinary circumstances. He lived under an oppressive colonial government and rebelled against it. An activist who spent 27 years in prison, Mandela helped free South Africa from apartheid and became the first black president of that country in 1994.

Mandela grew up in the land where satyagraha was born, and Gandhi's legacy was still very strong there. He became involved in politics as a university student and participated in demonstrations against the white minority government of South Africa, which denied rights to the black majority. He studied

> I want world sympathy in this battle of Right against Might.
>
> Gandhi
>
> M.K. Gandhi
>
> 5.4.30

Gandhi passed this note to the press so that they would convey his message to the world. Martin Luther King, Jr., employed many of the Mahatma's tactics to win public sympathy for his cause.

law and joined the African National Congress in 1942, becoming a major player in the anti-apartheid movement and, like Gandhi, representing for little or no pay many members of his race who could not afford to defend their legal rights. Although Mandela initially supported nonviolence, his views changed after the Sharpeville Massacre in 1960, when South African police opened fire on black protestors. Unlike Gandhi, Mandela and his colleagues in the ANC decided that armed

Nelson Mandela appears with former South African President F. W. de Klerk, who worked to free his country from apartheid and released Mandela from prison.

campaigns were necessary to bring about change. Mandela was eventually arrested for coordinating sabotage campaigns against the government. His imprisonment became a symbol of the injustice of colonial rule.

Perhaps the greatest impact of Gandhi's teachings on Mandela and the ANC party was that of tolerance. Mandela's party brought together Hindus, Muslims, Christians, and Jews. These diverse people were bound by a common goal—freedom from colonial rule. For his ability to find this "common ground," as he called it, Mandela was awarded in 1993 a special honor that Gandhi himself never received: the Nobel Peace Prize. In his acceptance speech, Mandela echoed Gandhi's words. He insisted that he was merely the representative of millions of people around the world who "recognized that an injury to one is an injury to all."

To those who remember him and to those who were born long after his death, Gandhi is a symbol of faith, peace, strength, and triumph over oppression. Several sites throughout India honor

> *"Countless human beings…had the nobility of spirit to stand in the path of tyranny and injustice.…They recognized that an injury to one is an injury to all…"*
>
> –Nelson Mandela, in his Nobel acceptance speech

117

his memory and are popular with visitors from around the world. They strive to preserve Gandhi's message, as well as document his rich life.

The Gandhi memorial at Raj Ghat attracts visitors from around the world, as well as dignitaries who wish to pay their respects to the "father of the nation."

Gandhi's birthplace in Porbandar is preserved as a national monument. The ashram he established in Ahmedabad still stands and makes handmade paper and spinning wheels. At Dandi Beach, there is a monument on the spot where Gandhi picked up salt from the sea in defiance of the salt laws. At Birla House in New Delhi, the site of Gandhi's assassination, visitors can see the exact spot where he fell to Godse's bullet. The Gandhi Memorial at Raj Ghat

is located by the banks of the River Jamuna where he was cremated, and an eternal flame burns there in his memory.

Beyond India, too, the world remembers the simple man in sandals and khadi who started a revolution. In the United States, a large sculpture of Gandhi was dedicated in 1990 at California State University, Fresno. In 1998, the Indian government donated a statue of Gandhi to the United States. The nine foot bronze figure—much taller than Gandhi in real life—was installed opposite India's embassy in Washington, D.C. Quotations by Gandhi are carved into the granite base. Gandhi's words made a lasting

The Mahatma works at his spinning wheel, which became a symbol of Indian independence.

mark, but he wanted his deeds to be remembered most: "My writings should be cremated with my body. What I have done will endure, not what I have said and written."

Indeed, the legacy of Gandhi's acts is still felt, particularly in India, where many of the religious, economic, and political wounds opened during the independence movement remain unhealed: the divide between Muslims and Hindus, the sad condition of untouchables, and the separation of India and Pakistan. There are more than one billion people in India today, millions of whom live in dire poverty. For all India's citizens, Gandhi's message of tolerance and compassion continues to have special meaning more than 50 years after his country freed itself from British rule.

Gandhi sacrificed himself as an individual to the greater causes of freedom and human rights. He gave up his possessions, time with his family, and ultimately, his life. In death, he became a symbol of the principles he had lived for: truth and nonviolence. He felt both were essential to attaining world peace. Gandhi knew it would take incredible strength for humanity to achieve this goal, but he thought the effort was necessary:

"We may never be strong enough to be entirely nonviolent, in thought, word, and deed. But we must keep nonviolence as our goal and make steady progress towards it.…The truth of a few will count. The untruth of millions will vanish even like chaff before a whiff of wind."

A simple, gentle, and fragile-looking man who grew large and powerful in people's hearts, Mahatma Gandhi understood the risk of peacefully opposing nations that were armed with weapons and overrun with abuse—but he was not afraid. From boyhood to death, he continued to find comfort in his faith and courage in the truth.

> *"The truth of a few will count. The untruth of millions will vanish even like chaff before a whiff of wind."*
>
> –Gandhi

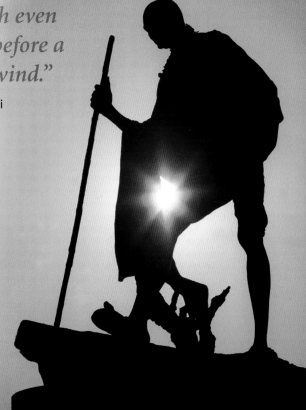

This monument to Gandhi in Madras shows the Mahatma forging ahead with great purpose, true to the spirit of his life.

Events in the Life of Mohandas Gandhi

October 2, 1869
Mohandas Gandhi is born in Porbandar, India.

May 1915
Gandhi founds ashram in Ahmedabad.

September 4, 1888
Gandhi sails to England to study law.

1906
Gandhi first uses the word "satyagraha" to describe his nonviolence campaign.

1883
Thirteen-year-old Mohandas marries Kasturba.

May–June, 1893
Gandhi experiences racial discrimination and vows to fight it.

1907–1914
The fight against the Black Act and General Smuts begins.

April 1893
Gandhi leaves for South Africa to act as legal consultant.

1917
Gandhi launches Champaran campaign for the rights of indigo workers.

March 10–18, 1922
Gandhi is arrested for sedition, charged, and sentenced to six years in prison.

September 1931
Gandhi and other delegates attend the Second Round Table Conference in England to discuss Dominion status for India.

January 13–18, 1948
Gandhi fasts for communal unity.

August 15, 1947
India celebrates independence.

August 1946
Gandhi opposes the partition of India.

September 1924
Gandhi fasts for Hindu-Muslim unity.

February 22, 1944
Kasturba dies in prison.

April 13, 1919
The Amritsar Massacre occurs after Gandhi calls off the hartal.

September 20–26, 1932
Gandhi fasts to oppose separate elections for untouchables.

August 1942
The Quit India campaign begins.

April 6, 1930
The Salt March inspires Indians to break salt laws.

January 30, 1948
Gandhi is assassinated by Hindu extremist Nathuram Godse.

Bibliography

Attenborough, Richard, ed. *The Words of Gandhi*. New York: Newmarket Press, 1982.

Brown, Judith M. *Gandhi: Prisoner of Hope*. New Haven and London: Yale University Press, 1989.

Collins, Larry and Dominique Lapierre. *Freedom at Midnight*. New York: HarperCollins, 1997.

Demi. *Gandhi*. New York: Margaret K. McElderry Books, 2001.

Gandhi, Mohandas K. *Gandhi An Autobiography: My Experiments with Truth*. Boston: Beacon Press, 1983.

Hunter, Nigel. *Gandhi*. New York: The Bookwright Press, 1987.

James, Lawrence. *Raj: The Making and Unmaking of British India*. New York: St. Martin's Press, 1997.

King, Martin Luther Jr. *The Autobiography of Martin Luther King, Jr*. New York: Warner Books, 2001.

Mandela, Nelson. *Long Walk to Freedom*. Boston: Little, Brown, 1994.

Severance, John B. *Gandhi: Great Soul*. New York: Clarion Books, 1997.

Shirer, William L. *Gandhi: A Memoir*. New York: Simon and Schuster, 1979.

Wilkinson, Philip. *Gandhi: The Young Protestor Who Founded a Nation*. Washington, D.C.: National Geographic, 2005.

Works Cited

Page 26: "I do not think caste should interfere…," *Autobiography*. p. 40

Page 29: "Everything was strange…," *Autobiography*, p. 45

Page 31: "achieve anything like rhythmic motion…," *Autobiography*, p. 51

Page 31: "If my character made a gentleman…," *Autobiography*, p. 51

Page 34: "But I say unto you…," *Autobiography*, p. 68

Page 37: "Never again shall I place myself…," *Autobiography*, p. 99

Page 40: "unwelcome visitor," *Autobiography*, p. 107-108

Page 42: "Should I fight for my rights…," *Autobiography*, p. 112

Page 45: "It is the first nail in our coffin," *Autobiography*, p. 139

Page 50: "If you wish to live…," *Autobiography*, p. 255

Page 51: "That the good of the individual…," *Autobiography*, p. 299

Page 59: "Not worthy to stand in the shoes…," www.mkgandhi.org/bio5000

Page 63: "As a law-abiding citizen…," *Autobiography*, p. 413

Page 68: "The time has come when…," www.nobelprize.org

Page 68: "Leaders were put under arrest…," *Autobiography*, p. 471

Page 74: "it is a million times better…," www.mkgandhi.org

Page 75: "I should have known…," *Gandhi: A Memoir*, p. 85

Page 75: "I do not ask for mercy…," *Gandhi: A Memoir*, p. 85

Page 76: "if in the course of events…," *Gandhi: A Memoir*, p. 90

Page 82: "If my letter makes no appeal…," *Gandhi: A Memoir*, p. 93-94

Acknowledgments

I am grateful to Prachi Dalal for her helpful comments and suggestions and to Alisha Niehaus at DK Publishing for her guidance throughout the project. John Searcy at DK was a thoughtful text editor. Thanks to Howard Kaplan for his support and to Peter, Nicholas, and Oliver for inspiration.

For Further Study

Visit www.mkgandhi.org and learn about Gandhi's life, work, and philosophy. The site is run by Gandhi organizations in India and offers material for students, researchers, and anyone interested in the Mahatma.

Browse www.mahatma.com and read some of Gandhi's speeches, letters, and articles. The site lists Gandhi ashrams in India, Gandhi museums and libraries in India, and institutes and centers throughout the world that carry on Gandhi's work.

Navigate through www.indianchild.com/history_of_india.htm, a site for parents and children that allows the user to investigate the history of India. Gandhi is profiled in the Freedom Fighters of India section.

Click on www.thekingcenter.com to see a site about Civil Rights leader Martin Luther King, Jr., who was inspired by Gandhi's message.

Search www.nelsonmandela.org, a site devoted to the ongoing work of Nelson Mandela and his effort to expand human freedom throughout the world. It contains a biography of Mandela, chronicles his work, and contains photographs.

Index

Picture Credits

The photographs in this book are used with permission and through the courtesy of (T=top;
B=bottom; L=left; R=right): Alamy Images: p.10 Network Photographers; p.32 ephotocorp; pp.42-43,
50B Dinodia Images; p.94 Robert Harding Picture Library; p.120 Tibor Bognor. AP/Wide World
Photos: pp.93, 106-107, 109, 113. Art Archive: pp.80, 88B Dagli Orti; p.123 TL. Art Resource: p.14
Erich Lessing; p.25 Scala. Bridgeman Art Library: p.11 British Museum; p.16 Illustrated London
News Picture Library; p.85 Bibliotheque Nationale. Corbis: pp.2-3, 23, 70 Hulton Deutsch; p.7
Historical Picture Archive; p.12 Macduff Everton; p.13 Dave Bartruff; p.17 Dagli Orti; p.28, 33
Corbis; p.51B, 66, 72-73, 82B, 83, 84, 85, 88T, 105, 123BL, 124-125, 126-127 Bettman; p.69T
Michael Freeman; p.79, 123TR Royalty Free; p.82T Michael Nicholson ; p.114 Flip Schulke; 116
Reuters. Dinodia Photo Library: pp.1, 18, 19T-B, 20, 21, 22, 24, 30, 31, 34, 35, 38, 39, 46T-B, 48-49T-
B, 50T, 52-53, 55, 58-59, 60, 61B, 67, 69B, 71B, 73, 74-75, 76T-B, 77, 81, 86, 89, 90, 95, 96, 97, 98, 100,
101, 101-102, 108, 110-111, 111, 115, 122TL-R, 123TC, 123BR. DK Publishing: pp.63, 118, 122BR.
Getty Images: pp.4-5, 6, 26-27, 29, 36, 40-41, 44, 47, 51TL, 61T, 87, 91, 92, 98-99, 122BL; pp.51B,
56, 78, 119 Time&Life Pictures. Image Works: pp.57, 65, 71T DPA; p.62 Science Museum/SSPL.
Link Picture Library: p.42. BORDER PICTURES: from left to right: Getty Images; Dinodia Picture
Library; Dinodia Picture Library; Dinodia Picture Library; Getty Images; Dinodia Picture Library;
Getty Images; Getty Images; DK Publishing; Corbis; Getty Images.

About the Author

Amy Pastan is a writer, editor, and producer of illustrated books for children and adults. She is the author of *DK Biography: Martin Luther King, Jr.* and *Eyewitness First Ladies.* Amy also served as photo editor for *The DK Children's Encyclopedia of American History.* She lives in Washington, D.C., with her husband, her two sons, and a pet snake.

Other DK Biographies you may enjoy:

Look what the critics are saying about DK Biography!

"…highly readable, worthwhile overviews for young people…"—*Booklist*

"This new series from the inimitable DK Publishing brings together the usual brilliant photography with a historian's approach to biography subjects."
—*Ingram Library Services*